CENTURY

OF

COLLAPSE

WHY CIVILIZATIONS FALL

by Andrew Strom

Revival School

Century of Collapse
Copyright © 2022 by Andrew Strom. All rights reserved.

No part of this publication may be reproduced, stored in a retrieval system, or transmitted in any form or by any means, electronic, mechanical, photocopying, recording, scanning, or otherwise, without the prior written permission of the author.

Limit of Liability/Disclaimer of Warranty: This publication is designed to provide accurate and authoritative information in regard to the subject matter covered. It is sold with the understanding that neither the author nor the publisher is engaged in rendering legal, investment, accounting or other professional services. While the publisher and author have used their best efforts in preparing this book, they make no representations or warranties with respect to the accuracy or completeness of the contents of this book. Neither the publisher nor the author shall be liable for any loss of profit or any other commercial damages, including but not limited to special, incidental, consequential, personal, or other damages.

'Century of Collapse – Why Civilizations Fall' – by Andrew Strom

1. Civilization – History. 2. Civilization – Philosophy. 3. Regression (Civilization). 4. Religion and civilization.

ISBN-13: 978-0-9831866-4-9

ISBN-10: 0-9831866-4-2

Printed in the United States of America

Published by: RevivalSchool

Wholesale distribution by Lightning Source, Inc.

CONTENTS

1. Demographic Death 1

2. The Fate of Empires 9

3. The Age of Decadence 17

4. The Death of Europe 35

5. An Empty Planet? 53

6. The Eastern Death Spiral 61

7. Japan's Epic Fall 71

8. The Mouse Utopia Experiments 81

9. China & the Asian Tigers.................................103

10. Crash of Civilizations 109

11. America's Last Hope 121

References & Quotations 135

CHAPTER ONE

DEMOGRAPHIC DEATH

War suddenly breaks out. Food and energy prices soar. Markets are in turmoil. Such monumental happenings dominate the news cycle – and rightly so. But beneath the surface even larger tectonic shifts are underway – shifts that will play out over decades rather than mere months. Tremors so great that even our very civilization itself may be at stake.

What if I told you that over the next 100 years, the once-great nations of Italy and Greece will lose more than half their populations? Millions and millions gone. And what if I told you that Japan will lose two-thirds of it's population over the same period (going from 125 million down to 40 million)? And that China – the great power that everyone fears – will also see its population halve over the same time frame?

Would you believe me if I said such things? Or would you write me off as some kind of crackpot – perhaps a Climate Change doomsayer, prophesying disaster? Actually, the cataclysm I am speaking of has nothing to do with global warming. In fact, any effects from climate change come on top of what I am predicting here.

We are headed for a century of collapse. This is utterly provable from facts and statistics that are commonly available around the globe. In fact, this entire process is already underway. In 100 years, Spain and Portugal will have lost two-thirds of their populations. Italy will be a shadow of its former self. South Korea will be an economic disaster zone. The "Asian tigers" will be no more. China and Japan will be in a state of complete societal disarray. And even North America will be deeply affected.

But how can I make these predictions with such confidence, you ask? How can I be so sure? Isn't the future, by it's very nature, difficult to pin down?

I make these statements the same way an insurance assessor knows that next year in a particular country there will be 175,000 auto accidents. He has the data for all previous years. He knows the trends. He knows they barely change from year to year – maybe a few thousand up or down. He has all the data at his fingertips and he can tell you with pretty high accuracy what the accident rate will be in that country five years down the line. Insurance companies make these kinds of predictions all the time. And if they were not accurate they would likely go out of business.

LET THE NUMBERS SPEAK

Similar to insurance companies, we are in the "births and deaths" business here. And these statistics are among the most meticulously-kept by virtually every nation across the globe. We have decades and decades of data. We know the trends. We know the birthrates. We know the death rates. We can predict all kinds of things.

For instance, I can tell you with a great deal of accuracy how many 36-year-olds will be living in the nation of Australia in December 2052. This is because all those people have already been born. In fact, most of them were born in a single year – 2016. So for the year 2052 we simply take that number and adjust it a bit to account for early deaths and immigration, etc. And voila! A pretty precise reading of the number of 36-year-olds living in 2052 – years and years before it actually happens.

That is the power of demographics (the study of populations). And thus the saying, "Demography is destiny." Your nation's fate is hugely decided by the births, deaths and migrations of its people. And when we know those figures, we can know a great deal about what lies ahead.

ALARM FOR THIS CENTURY

So what do the numbers indicate for the next one hundred years? They say we are headed for the most alarming demographic cliff-edge in history. In fact, we are already going over it. They say that Western Europe will suffer a collapse from which it will not recover. They show that Eastern Europe is to enter a state of social and economic ruin. And they say that the whole of East Asia is bound for demographic and economic calamity.[1]

The populations of entire regions will literally melt away. There will be no developed or semi-developed nation on earth that will escape this cataclysm unscathed. And that includes North America.[2]

"But how can you say such things?" comes the cry. "How can this even be possible? We've been told that we're in the midst of a population explosion! That it's overpopulation that is the problem – not population collapse. Everything you're telling us goes right against the grain of all that we've been told."

Well, I guess that's what happens when you listen to Hollywood filmmakers, sci-fi writers, sensationalists and media pundits who know little of real demographics. When you listen to actual experts – the top demographers – you get an entirely different picture.

THOSE WHO TRULY KNOW

What we learn when we talk to actual demographers and PhDs is that the entire developed world is in the midst of the greatest demographic slowdown in recorded history. And we are decades into it. This is not a new thing. The full effects are now just coming into play.

So is there anyplace that is actually experiencing a population explosion? Yes – Africa. It is Africa that is the true home of the population bomb. Virtually everywhere else is home to a population "bust" of monumental proportions – that is only now beginning to bite. And it is about to get much, much worse.

This is the great misunderstanding – the real reason why everyone is so confused on this issue. We have completely failed to communicate that the "explosion" in population has almost all been confined to the developing world and the poorest countries. None of the richer nations have any kind of "explosion" going on – at least not since the 1960s. It has all been a total misunderstanding – and a very damaging one at that.

Little wonder that the *New York Times* listed Overpopulation as "one of the myths of the 20th century" in its January 1, 2000 *Millennium Edition*.[3] That was years ago, but the message still doesn't seem to have gotten through. The power of this "overpopulation" fable is so incredibly strong. We still see it popping up in movies to this day.

In July 2020 the *Lancet* published a study put out by Washington University showing that, due to the constant decline in birthrates worldwide, the peak in global population is now projected to occur in 2064 – at well bellow ten billion. That is just forty years away! This study uses the best and latest statistics from around the world. And please note that the peak for developed nations is set to occur much earlier.[4]

The *New York Times* described the study as having "major economic and political implications." According to the *Times*, "The study asserted that the global population could peak at 9.7 billion by 2064 — nearly four decades earlier — and decline to 8.8 billion by 2100... and the populations of at least 23 countries, including Japan, Thailand, Italy and Spain, could shrink by more than 50 percent."[5]

Well-known billionaire Elon Musk has been sounding the alarm on this issue for years. And so has renowned geopolitical analyst Peter Zeihan. But again, hardly anyone seems to be listening.

SELECTIVE HEARING

Of course, hundreds of newspapers around the world have printed articles on this topic in recent decades. Books, features and news items that quote true experts have been published regularly, yet few seem to grasp the danger. Hollywood trumps all. Science fiction carries the day. *Blade Runner* says "overpopulation" so it must be true. Isn't that the way of it?

Let's take a look at some recent headlines on this topic from across the globe. The message is unequivocal:

-"The depopulation timebomb facing the West is about to explode." *(The Telegraph).*

-"Global Fertility Rate: A Population Crash Is Coming." *(Bloomberg).*

-"UK natural population set to start to decline by 2025." *(Financial Times).*

-"Heading for population collapse?" *(The Week).*

-"Baby Bust: China's Looming Demographic Disaster." *(The Spectator).*

-"Long Slide Looms for World Population, With Sweeping Ramifications." *(NYT).*

It is time for us to listen to the real facts. They are by no means hidden or difficult to get hold of. A few taps of a laptop keyboard are enough to open up an entire universe of statistics and trends in this field. But we have not been listening. And thus when catastrophe overtakes us and our civilization, we are liable to be left speechless in open-mouthed wonder. Not a fitting end for a supposedly "advanced" and knowledgeable culture.

In the following chapters we will not just be looking at what is causing these declines and how bad things might get, but we will also be looking at civilizations in general – and what causes them to fall. History has a great deal to teach us about the state of empires before they self-destruct – and the signs to look for that give advance warning of the end.

We would do well to ascertain whether these alarm bells are ringing for our own culture, and what might be done – if anything – to avert disaster before it is too late.

CHAPTER TWO

THE FATE OF EMPIRES

It was the renowned historian Arnold J. Toynbee, who said: "Great civilizations die from suicide, not by murder." Toynbee, who had studied the rise and fall of 23 major empires throughout history, also wrote: "There is nothing to prevent our Western civilization from following historical precedent, if it chooses, by committing social suicide... The present Western ascendancy in the world is certain not to last." [1]

So what are the signs of a civilization on the verge of collapse? Are there stages that civilizations go through – a life-cycle of rise and fall – that we can learn from in order to avoid such a fate? What are these pitfalls and how do we identify them before it's too late?

Of course, many books and essays have been published on this topic over the years. One particularly notable paper was put out by Sir John Glubb, a British commander, scholar and author, in 1978. It was entitled, *The Fate of Empires*, and gave a broad overview of different stages that he believed all empires or civilizations go through.

Like Toynbee, Glubb had spent years studying various civilizations down through history – especially the major ones. As he wrote in his paper, "The experiences of the human race have been recorded, in more or less detail, for some four thousand years... We seem to discover the same patterns constantly repeated under widely differing conditions...

everything that is occurring around us has happened again and again before."[2]

One of the most interesting points Glubb made was that the average empire seemed to last roughly ten generations – or 250 years. This gave each one enough time to reach the pinnacle of its success and prosperity, only to then fall into slow decline and collapse. Below is the table he included to illustrate this point:

THE NATION	RISE AND FALL	DURATION
Assyria	859-612 B.C.	247 yrs
Persia	538-330 B.C.	208 yrs
Greece	331-100 B.C.	231 yrs
Roman Republic	260-27 B.C.	233 yrs
Roman Empire	27 B.C. – A.D. 180	207 yrs
Arab Empire	A.D. 634-880	246 yrs
Mameluke Empire	1250-1517	267 yrs
Ottoman Empire	1320-1570	250 yrs
Spain	1500-1750	250 yrs
Romanov Russia	1682-1916	234 yrs
Britain	1700-1950	250 yrs

Glubb continues: "In a surprising manner, 250 years emerges as the average length of national greatness... This average has not varied for 3,000 years." Of course, Glubb himself was very aware of the obvious question this raises: "What then, we may ask, can have been the factor which caused such an extraordinary similarity in the duration of empires...?"

Glubb's own response was that it has something to do with the number of generations that 250 years represents: "The human 'generation' [is] a period of about twenty-five years. Thus a period of 250 years would represent about ten generations of people."[3]

Clearly, what Glubb is getting at here is that ten generations is just enough time for a great power to rise to its absolute peak of influence and wealth – only to have its very success and prosperity become the chief cause of its decline and fall. The fact that this cycle so often repeats itself over a similar number of generations is certainly surprising, but perhaps it just goes to show that human behavior is not as random or unpredictable as we might have thought.

From what Glubb discovered, it appears that the first half of the life-cycle of any civilization is spent industriously building and fighting its way to the top. But then it becomes so prosperous and wealthy that the latter half is spent undermining virtually everything the empire was built on in the first place. The rot slowly takes over.

(Of course, people from the United States often take great interest in this "250 year" concept – since the 250 year anniversary of their own founding is due in 2026).

A REPEATING DOWNFALL

In his paper, Glubb goes on to outline the different stages that each of these civilizations seemed to go through – from their birth right through to their demise. Below are the six stages he identified:

(1) The Age of Pioneers (outburst).

(2) The Age of Conquests.

(3) The Age of Commerce.

(4) The Age of Affluence.

(5) The Age of Intellect.

(6) The Age of Decadence.

When we consider our own civilization, there is no denying that it is the final three of these stages that are the most relevant, since we can clearly see abundant evidence of them in our own culture over the last 100 years.

Grubb writes: "There does not appear to be any doubt that money is the agent which causes the decline of this strong, brave and self-confident people. The decline in courage, enterprise and a sense of duty is, however, gradual. The first direction in which wealth injures the nation is a moral one. Money replaces honour and adventure as the objective of the best young men. Moreover, men do not normally seek to make money for their country or their community, but for themselves.

"Gradually, and almost imperceptibly, the Age of Affluence silences the voice of duty. The object of the young and the ambitious is no longer fame, honour or service, but cash. Education undergoes the same gradual transformation. No longer do schools aim at producing brave patriots ready to serve their country. Parents and students alike seek the educational qualifications which will command the highest salaries."

Grubb continues: "That which we may call the High Noon of the nation covers the period of transition from the Age of Conquests to the Age of Affluence: the age of Augustus in Rome, that of Harun al-Rashid in Baghdad... or of Queen Victoria in Britain. Perhaps we might add the age of Woodrow Wilson in the United States.

"All these periods reveal the same characteristics. The immense wealth accumulated in the nation dazzles the onlookers. Enough of the ancient virtues of courage, energy and patriotism survive to enable the state successfully to defend its frontiers. But, beneath the surface, greed for money is gradually replacing duty and public service. Indeed the change might be summarised as being from service to selfishness."[4]

HIGHER EDUCATION

Next up, after the *Age of Affluence* has dominated for some time, comes what Glubb calls the *Age of Intellect*. Here is how he describes it: "The great wealth of the nation is no longer needed to supply the mere necessities, or even the luxuries of life. Ample funds are available also for the pursuit of knowledge... colleges and universities. It is remarkable with what regularity this phase follows on that of wealth, in empire after empire, divided by many centuries.

"In the eleventh century... During the reign of Malik Shah, the building of universities and colleges became a passion. Whereas a small number of universities in the great cities had sufficed the years of Arab glory, now a university sprang up in every town. In our own lifetime, we have witnessed the same phenomenon in the U.S.A. and Britain. When these nations were at the height of their glory, Harvard, Yale, Oxford and Cambridge seemed to meet their needs. Now almost every city has its university." [5]

Glubb continues: "The spread of knowledge seems to be the most beneficial of human activities, and yet every period of decline is characterised by this expansion of intellectual activity... The Age of Intellect is accompanied by surprising advances in natural science.

"In the ninth century, for example, in the age of Mamun, the Arabs measured the circumference of the earth with remarkable accuracy. Seven centuries were to pass before Western Europe discovered that the world was not flat. Less than fifty years after the amazing scientific discoveries under Mamun, the Arab Empire collapsed. Wonderful and beneficent as was the progress of science, it did not save the empire from chaos."

Glubb goes on: "As in the case of the Athenians, intellectualism leads to discussion, debate and argument, such as is typical of the Western nations today... Perhaps the most dangerous by-product of the Age of Intellect is the unconscious growth of the idea that the human brain can solve the problems of the world... The impression that the situation can be saved by mental cleverness, without unselfishness or human self-dedication, can only lead to collapse."[6]

CIVIL STRIFE

The Fate of Empires continues: "Another remarkable and unexpected symptom of national decline is the intensification of internal political hatreds. One would have expected that, when the survival of the nation became precarious, political factions would drop their rivalry and stand shoulder-to-shoulder to save their country.

"In the fourteenth century, the weakening empire of Byzantium was threatened, and indeed dominated, by the Ottoman Turks. The situation was so serious that one would have expected every subject of Byzantium to abandon his personal interests and to stand with his compatriots in a last desperate attempt to save the country. The reverse occurred. The Byzantines spent the last fifty years of their history in fighting one another in repeated civil wars, until the Ottomans moved in and administered the coup de grâce...

"We are fortunate if these rivalries are fought out in Parliament, but sometimes such hatreds are carried into the streets, or into industry in the form of strikes, demonstrations, boycotts and similar activities. True to the normal course followed by nations in decline, internal differences are not reconciled in an attempt to save the nation. On the contrary, internal rivalries become more acute, as the nation becomes weaker."

Glubb goes on: "One of the oft-repeated phenomena of great empires is the influx of foreigners to the capital city... It is the wealth of the great cities which draws the immigrants... Once more it may be emphasised that I do not wish to convey the impression that immigrants are inferior to older stocks. They are just different, and they thus tend to introduce cracks and divisions."[7]

Glubb's paper continues: "The striking features in the pageant of empire are: (a) the extraordinary exactitude with which these stages have followed one another, in empire after empire, over centuries or even millennia; and (b) the fact that the successive changes seem to represent mere changes in popular fashion—new fads and fancies which sweep away public opinion without logical reason. At first, popular enthusiasm is devoted to military glory, then to the accumulation of wealth and later to the acquisition of academic fame."[8]

And now we come to the final phase – the one that Glubb referred to as the *Age of Decadence*. Of all the stages that he outlined, this is the one that most clearly reflects the current state of our own civilization. All the signs are there. As Glubb himself wrote: "'The only thing we learn from history,' it has been said, 'is that men never learn from history', a sweeping generalisation perhaps, but one which the chaos in the world today goes far to confirm."

It is in the following chapter that we will examine what history has to teach us about this terminal stage in the course of empires – and the direct similarities to our own time and culture.

CHAPTER THREE

THE AGE OF DECADENCE

As we have seen, it is the human response to comfort and riches that make a lot of these 'phases' of civilization so predictable. As wealth and influence flow into the new power over a period of generations, so the rot sets in. This is why the exact same stages can be seen across empires and kingdoms vastly separated in time and space. The human response to prosperity and success always bears similar fruit. It is an undermining force. But after a time even the wealth itself, for the average citizen, begins to stagnate or recede.

Speaking of this cycle of decay, Sir John Glubb writes: "As the nation declines in power and wealth, a universal pessimism gradually pervades the people, and itself hastens the decline... no disasters could shake the resolution of the early Romans. Yet, in the later stages of Roman decline, the whole empire was deeply pessimistic, thereby sapping its own resolution.

"Frivolity is the frequent companion of pessimism. Let us eat, drink and be merry, for tomorrow we die. The resemblance between various declining nations in this respect is truly surprising. The Roman mob, we have seen, demanded free meals and public games. Gladiatorial shows, chariot races and athletic events were their passion.

"In the Byzantine Empire the rivalries of the Greens and the Blues in the hippodrome attained the importance of a major crisis. Judging by the time and space allotted to them in the Press and television, football and baseball are the activities which today chiefly interest the public in Britain and the United States respectively.

"The heroes of declining nations are always the same—the athlete, the singer or the actor. The word 'celebrity' today is used to designate a comedian or a football player, not a statesman, a general, or a literary genius."[1]

THE POP SINGERS OF BAGHDAD

Now comes one of the most astounding sections of Glubb's entire discourse – his description of the decline of the Arab empire in the ninth century AD: "In the first half of the ninth century, Baghdad enjoyed its High Noon as the greatest and the richest city in the world. In 861, however, the reigning Khalif (caliph), Mutawakkil, was murdered by his Turkish mercenaries, who set up a military dictatorship, which lasted for some thirty years. During this period the empire fell apart...

"The works of the contemporary historians of Baghdad in the early tenth century are still available. They deeply deplored the degeneracy of the times in which they lived, emphasising particularly the indifference to religion, the increasing materialism and the laxity of sexual morals. They lamented also the corruption of the officials of the government and the fact that politicians always seemed to amass large fortunes while they were in office.

"The historians commented bitterly on the extraordinary influence acquired by popular singers over young people, resulting in a decline in sexual morality. The 'pop' singers of Baghdad accompanied their erotic songs on the lute, an instrument resembling the modern guitar. In the second half of the tenth century, as a result, much obscene sexual language came increasingly into use, such as would not have been tolerated in an earlier age. Several khalifs issued orders banning 'pop' singers from the capital, but within a few years they always returned."

An astonished Glubb continues: "When I first read these contemporary descriptions of tenth-century Baghdad, I could scarcely believe my eyes. I told myself that this must be a joke! The descriptions might have been taken out of The Times today. The resemblance of all the details was especially breathtaking—the break-up of the empire, the abandonment of sexual morality, the 'pop' singers with their guitars... I would not venture to attempt an explanation! There are so many mysteries about human life which are far beyond our comprehension."[2]

THE SEXUAL REVOLUTION

Of course, if we are looking for the beginning of this *Age of Decadence* in our own civilization, many would point to the sexual revolution of the 1960s and 1970s as a starting point. But what some may not realize is that this was as much a scientific revolution as it was a social and cultural one. The whole thing was underpinned by a scientific breakthrough that had occurred during the 1950s.

In fact, the 1950s can easily be seen as the very peak of our own *Age of Affluence*. These were the years of the post-war "baby boom" when America discovered suburban living and the middle classes came to enjoy comforts barely dreamed-of before. Prosperity came to the masses, married life was at its peak, and it was not uncommon for families to have four children or more. But all that was about to change – in ways that seemed so innocent at first. This is where we see the first portents of a "population crash" entering Western life.

Since 1953 a team led by Margaret Sanger and Dr. John Rock of the United States had been developing a pill that women could take to prevent pregnancy. In 1956 they began clinical trials and in 1960 the FDA approved this new birth-control pill for married women everywhere. The effect was immediate – and startling. The birthrate in America began to plummet downwards. If you can imagine the chart of a stock market crash, the birthrate in the Western world looked similar to that. It literally fell off a cliff.[3]

It was the separation of sex from reproduction that had changed everything. That is what this pill did. For the first time in human history, it was now possible for a couple to have sex and yet not concern themselves with the possibility of pregnancy. And little did anyone know that when you change this one fundamental fact of nature, everything else about human society changes irrevocably.

Of course, to even discuss the "pill" in this way is to invite scorn and derision from across the board. In our society this is a sacred cow of the highest order. Only a politically incorrect imbecile would even ask questions about it – so the thinking goes. Well, get ready for a lot more political incorrectness in this book. Unless we discuss such things openly and honestly, it is simply impossible to comprehend the crisis that lies ahead – or the reasons behind it.

THE WORLD SHIFTS

In 2014, *Wall Street Journal* reporter Jonathan Eig released his book, *The Birth of the Pill: How Four Crusaders Reinvented Sex and Launched a Revolution.* During an interview with NPR, Eig talked about why he had wanted to write the book: "I was listening to a rabbi's sermon — this was maybe five or six years ago — and he began by saying that the birth control pill may have been the most important invention of the 20th century.

"My immediate reaction was, "That's nuts. That can't possibly be. I can think of six things off the top of my head that seemed more important than that." But it stayed with me. I kept thinking about it. A couple of years went by and I was still thinking about it. His case was that it had changed more than just science, more than just medicine. It had changed human dynamics. It had changed the way men and women get along in the world." [4]

By the mid-1960s this new contraceptive pill was approved for all women – not just those who were married – and the stage was now set for one of the greatest shakeups in sexual mores that any society has ever seen. The sexual revolution was on – a huge cultural watershed throughout the Western world. But it is important to remember that a lot of this could not have happened without the invention of the "pill." [5]

By 1973 the birthrate in most Western nations (including the USA) had plunged below the replacement rate (the rate needed to keep the population stable). Without immigration, most of these countries would now begin shrinking away. And it has largely been the same ever since. (In fact, today most developed nations have birthrates that are at record lows never seen before).

So what was the result of this "revolution"? Marriage rates tumbled, divorce rates skyrocketed, the number of children growing up without a father multiplied. Family formation and the general happiness of women tanked.[6] A whole raft of social pathologies, drug use and mental health issues proliferated. And this is only scratching the surface of what has occurred in the decades since. The West is no longer the place it used to be.

But of course, not all of this can be laid at the feet of the "pill." That was the scientific breakthrough which simply set the scene for what was to follow. The revolution itself was a social and cultural one. But we need to remember the scientific underpinnings that allowed it to take place.

THE BRITISH INVASION

Earlier we quoted Sir John Glubb's description of the "pop singers" of Baghdad and the decline in sexual morality that occurred during the fall of that empire. As most of us know, the exact same thing happened during the 1960s and 1970s in our own civilization. (In fact, it is still happening today).

Before we discuss this further, I just want to note that I am a musician myself, and someone who enjoys a wide range of modern music. But that cannot be allowed to detract from some of the things I need to highlight here. As I said before, in order to fully understand the state of our civilization today, we can't avoid touching on subjects that some will find objectionable. I'm sorry, but that's just the way it is. We either face the facts or bury our head in the sand.

As is well known, the British group *The Beatles* hit number one on the American music charts for the first time in early 1964. Thus began what is referred to as the "British Invasion" of pop groups from England dominating the charts (and the young minds) of the Western world for more than a decade. And crucially, this was the decade at the heart of the sexual revolution – the period when it really took off.

Mind you, it might be worth considering the words of *Beatle* George Harrison regarding this time: "They used us as an excuse to go mad, the world did, and then blamed it on us." Despite Harrison's protestations, however, I believe there is something important about the "British" connection to what took place during those years.

You see, Britain at this time was itself a "fallen" empire – an empire much further along the 'decline curve' than America or some of the other Western nations. And I think this was particularly true in the area of religious faith.

Overall, Britain was much more cynical and much further-gone in its disengagement from Christianity, in my view. You can see it in the statistics and you can even see it in many of the interviews with pop stars from the period – including the notorious one where John Lennon claimed *The Beatles* were "bigger than Jesus." In fact, that whole episode is a great example of what I am talking about.

WORDS OF DECLINE

In March 1966, during an interview with journalist Maureen Cleave for the *London Evening Standard,* Lennon made the following statement: "Christianity will go. It will vanish and shrink. I needn't argue with that; I'm right and I will be proved right. We're more popular than Jesus now; I don't know which will go first – rock 'n' roll or Christianity. Jesus was all right but his disciples were thick and ordinary. It's them twisting it that ruins it for me." [7]

In Britain this comment caused barely a ripple when it was published. Christianity there had already been in steady decline for years by this time and no-one in the UK was particularly surprised at the world's most successful pop group making such statements – obnoxious though they might seem.

But in America it was a different story. Evangelical Christianity there was still in a healthy state, with preachers like Billy Graham and Oral Roberts being some of the most respected leaders in the nation. When John Lennon's comments were republished in the U.S., a giant furor erupted. All over the country, record-burnings of *Beatles* albums ensued. Shock, anger and reproach poured in from every side.

Before *The Beatles'* next tour of America, a reluctant John Lennon was forced to issue a halfhearted apology for his statements. This tour would prove to be their last – and it was undertaken with a real sense of nervousness and trepidation after all the controversy. However, the British domination of the music charts (and the young minds) of the Western world would still go on, virtually undiminished. The youth revolution had many years to run yet.

SPREADING DECAY

As I said earlier, what this British invasion meant was that an "already-declined" power could get to dominate the thinking and values of the youth of the West during a truly crucial decade. And this was to have an extremely significant impact, in my view. For the Christian faith and this new sexual revolution were totally at odds with one another. And thus, for many of the young "pop" leaders to come from a place where Christianity was dying made it far easier for them to undermine it.

Can anyone imagine a major American band pioneering "Satanic Rock" during this period? I certainly can't. Not in America. Not in 1967 or 1968. But in Britain they could get away with it – and then spread it around the world. When major British act *The Rolling Stones* released the album, *Their Satanic Majesties Request* in 1967 and their song, *Sympathy for the Devil* in 1968, the effect was revolutionary. Little surprise, then, that almost all the early Heavy Metal and Satanic Rock bands came out of Britain.

During the ten-year period around 1965 to 1975 (the height of the sexual revolution) it was British bands that largely predominated. First it was pop, then rock, then drugged-out psychedelia, then Metal, then the androgynous "bisexual" tones of Glam Rock and so on. The siren-call of decline was blasting out of every teenager's radio across the Western world.

About the only place that could compete with British influence during this period was the U.S. port city of San Francisco – which contributed hard drugs and hippy "free love" to the mix. But as I said, it was the fact that Christianity was in such serious decline in Britain that I believe had the greatest impact. It allowed the British bands to really "push the envelope" of social and cultural norms – and to lead the youth of the whole world down the same rebellious path.

FAITH EBBING AWAY

Speaking of this loss of faith that occurs during an *Age of Decadence,* Sir John Glubb writes: "The Age of Conquests often had some kind of religious atmosphere, which implied heroic self-sacrifice for the cause. But this spirit of dedication was slowly eroded in the Age of Commerce by the action of money. People make money for themselves, not for their country. Thus periods of affluence gradually dissolved the spirit of service."

Glubb continues: "In due course, selfishness permeated the community... Then, as we have seen, came the period of pessimism with the accompanying spirit of frivolity and sensual indulgence, by-products of despair. It was inevitable at such times that men should look back yearningly to the days of 'religion', when the spirit of self-sacrifice was still strong enough to make men ready to give and to serve, rather than to snatch.

"But while despair might permeate the greater part of the nation, others achieved a new realisation of the fact that only readiness for self-sacrifice could enable a community to survive. Some of the greatest saints in history lived in times of national decadence, raising the banner of duty and service against the flood of depravity and despair."[8]

THE GREAT OVERTHROW

So what were the aspects of Western life that came under attack from the proponents of the sexual revolution of the sixties? Well, it was basically anything that was seen as repressing the base urges of the young. Every authority, every moral code, every institution, every sexual or societal norm in existence – all were to be challenged and if necessary, overthrown. Every restriction on "total freedom" was to be obliterated.

At heart it was a utopian movement of peace and free love – permissiveness, hedonism and sexual liberation. Every gender role and stereotype was to be questioned, every moral or familial restriction torn down. As time went on, however, the movement became more and more saturated with heavy drugs. And the effects of these ideas on the family unit and on marriage across the Western world became more and more deleterious. Before long it became clear that this was an attack on the very fabric of civilization itself.

And yet, since this was basically a revolution among the young, it was very difficult for older people to have any say in slowing it down. The thing was a rolling tsunami and it was almost impossible to stop.

The effect on the black community in America was particularly tragic. (The poorest often suffer worst). Before 1960, a large majority of black women had been married before giving birth. Today, an astounding 72 percent of all black children are born out of wedlock.[9] Gang violence and drug addiction have skyrocketed. In study after study, fatherlessness has been linked to poverty, crime and other bad outcomes for children. All for the sake of a sexual revolution led by the elite few.

CHANGING GENDER NORMS

In what has to be one of the most controversial sections of *The Fate of Empires,* Sir John Glubb writes: "An increase in the influence of women in public life has often been associated with national decline. The later Romans complained that, although Rome ruled the world, women ruled Rome. In the tenth century, a similar tendency was observable in the Arab Empire, the women demanding admission to the professions hitherto monopolised by men...

"Many women practised law, while others obtained posts as university professors. There was an agitation for the appointment of female judges, which, however, does not appear to have succeeded. Soon after this period, government and public order collapsed, and foreign invaders overran the country. The resulting increase in confusion and violence made it unsafe for women to move unescorted in the streets, with the result that this feminist movement collapsed."[10]

Of course, the rise of feminism has also been a big part of the sexual revolution in our own culture. But we have taken this "gender" issue a lot further than any previous empire ever dreamed of. In 2021 the International Olympic Committee announced that there will no longer be a "testosterone test" for biological males wanting to compete as females in the Olympics. And the U.S. Justice Department has ruled it "unconstitutional" to prevent biological males from competing in women's sport if they so prefer.

In practice, what this has meant is that male athletes can simply announce themselves as a "woman," take testosterone-reducing drugs for a year and then begin competing as a female. Recently a biological-male swimmer who competed for U-Penn's male swim team swapped to the women's team and started breaking all the female swim records across the country. A number of women athletes, faced with this situation, began talking about quitting their sport, since there was now very little chance of winning. [11]

Where all this will end is anyone's guess. But one thing is sure: It is slowly destroying the sporting landscape that women spent years building up. What the verdict of history will be, one can only imagine.

ANTI-RELIGION

As we have discussed, proponents of the sexual revolution recognized Christianity as one of largest obstacles to their goal of "total liberation" from the very beginning. Though the Christian faith had proven a tremendous force for good across many generations, it did contain moral values and strictures that were completely at odds with this new "free love" movement. And thus it would have to go.

However, after the huge furor over John Lennon's comments in 1966, the 'pop' leaders knew they had to be a lot more subtle. Thus we almost never see a direct attack on Christianity by any of these leaders ever again. From now on their undermining of Christian values would be strongly implied, but never openly stated. They became masters at walking the very edge of the line – constantly pushing the envelope.

In 1967, the four *Beatles,* along with British pop singers Mick Jagger and Marianne Faithfull, went to Wales to sit publicly at the feet of Indian guru Maharishi Mahesh Yogi, openly embracing his message. This received front-page coverage across the Western world, and every youthful follower of *The Beatles* sat up and took notice.

The next year, *The Beatles* traveled to Rishikesh in northern India to take part in a Transcendental Meditation (TM) training course at the ashram of the Maharishi. This time they were accompanied by British pop singer Donovan plus Mike Love from the *Beach Boys,* along with actress Mia Farrow and others. Again, this received tremendous media attention across the globe.

There is no question that this was the beginning of what is now called the "New Age" movement – a convenient new faith where you can pick and choose whatever spiritual beliefs feel good to you. No more pesky morals or restrictions. An amorphous, vaguely Eastern set of beliefs for those who want to be "spiritual" but not religious. It is the kind of faith that lets you sleep with anyone at any time, a faith perfectly tailored for the sexual revolution. And that is no coincidence.

Surely *The Beatles* knew that millions of their young acolytes would follow them into these Eastern philosophies when they made such a big public deal of them? Absolutely. They had to know.

For years afterwards, George Harrison publicly flaunted his close ties with the *Hare Krishna* movement, and New Age-type influences were all the rage across the pop and rock industry. This had an absolutely enormous effect on the belief systems of the Western world – effects that are still with us today.

In 1971, John Lennon released his song *Imagine,* probably the most popular tune he ever recorded. The song begins with the words, *"Imagine there's no heaven, It's easy if you try."* It also invites listeners to *"Imagine there's no countries... And no religion, too."* BMI named it one of the 100 most performed songs of the twentieth century. More than 200 other artists have covered or performed the song, including Madonna, Stevie Wonder, Lady Gaga, Elton John and Diana Ross. [12]

WITHOUT MOORINGS

A lot of people probably wonder why we live in a world today that is so devoid of purpose and meaning. It is a world without deep foundations, with values so shallow as to be almost meaningless. Our culture provides nothing to stand on, no core foundation on which to build your life. All is shifting sand – materialist and consumerist in the extreme. Nothing deeper.

Little wonder that despair is rampant among our young. And little wonder that suicide, drug abuse and depression are at record levels across the developed world. We only need to look to the days of the sexual revolution to find the reason. Faith has been abandoned. Our deep moorings have been overthrown. If you want to know why today's young people are so spiritually rudderless – why there is such confusion and lack of purpose – this is the place to look.

Of course, it was not only the musicians and singers who were propagating these ideas. They were joined by a long list of allies – especially in education and the media. A whole new generation of young filmmakers arose in the late 1960s and early 1970s who were just as keen as anyone to overthrow the old norms. Everyone in media knew that "sex sells," so it wasn't long before they were joined by every television network in existence. Even TV newsrooms became totally subsumed. And a lot of the most influential universities and colleges had been in on this revolution from the beginning.

The whole thing became a propaganda juggernaut – an unstoppable media *blitzkrieg*. The "long march" through the institutions of the West had only just begun. And it is still going today. Joseph Goebbels himself could scarcely have dreamed up a more dazzling propaganda campaign than the one the West has been subjected to over the last sixty years. It is staggering in size and scope – it really is.

Some people wonder why conservatives in our culture have been going to such political extremes in recent times. The reason is simple. They have been losing the culture war for sixty years – and they know it. Losing for that long makes people desperate. And angry. Unsurprisingly, such anger leads to all kinds of drastic choices and decisions – some of them potentially unwise. But that is where we are today. Desperation is never cool or collected. And it is destabilizing the politics of much of the Western world. Left vs. Right is getting nasty.

You could almost say the sexual revolution has been too successful for its own good. But isn't that always the way? To repeat the words of Sir John Glubb: "The heroes of declining nations are always the same—the athlete, the singer or the actor... Past empires show almost every possible variation of political system, but all go through the same procedure from the Age of Pioneers through Conquest, Commerce, Affluence to decline and collapse."

THE INEVITABLE END

Like other historians, Glubb notes that the end-stage of a civilization is often accompanied by a series of economic crises. Speaking of the ninth-century Arab empire, Glubb writes: "The disorders following the military takeover in 861, and the loss of the empire, had played havoc with the economy. At such a moment, it might have been expected that everyone would redouble their efforts to save the country from bankruptcy, but nothing of the kind occurred. Instead, at this moment of declining trade and financial stringency, the people of Baghdad introduced a five-day week."

Glubb continues: "It may perhaps be incorrect to picture the welfare state as the high-water mark of human attainment. It may merely prove to be one more regular milestone in the life-story of an ageing and decrepit empire... The impression that it will always be automatically rich causes the declining empire to spend lavishly on its own benevolence, until such time as the economy collapses, the universities are closed and the hospitals fall into ruin."[13]

Glubb goes on: "Decadence is a moral and spiritual disease, resulting from too long a period of wealth and power, producing cynicism, decline of religion, pessimism and frivolity. The citizens of such a nation will no longer make an effort to save themselves, because they are not convinced that anything in life is worth saving...

"Decadence is marked by: Defensiveness; Pessimism; Materialism; Frivolity; An influx of foreigners; The Welfare State; A weakening of religion... Decadence is due to: Too long a period of wealth and power; Selfishness; Love of money; The loss of a sense of duty."

As his musings on this subject draw to a close, Glubb continues: "In spite of the endless variety and the infinite complications of human life, a general pattern does seem to emerge from these considerations. It reveals many successive empires covering some 3,000 years, as having followed similar stages of development and decline, and as having, to a surprising degree, 'lived' lives of very similar length... In a surprising manner, 250 years emerges as the average length of national greatness. This average has not varied for 3,000 years. Does it represent ten generations?"[14]

Earlier in this book we quoted Arnold Toynbee as saying that great civilizations die "not by murder, but by suicide." In coming chapters we will be looking at countries around the world that are currently committing suicide at a national level – and whether anything can be done to stop the rot.

CHAPTER FOUR

THE DEATH OF EUROPE

If there was any part of the world that fully imbibed every aspect of the sexual revolution alongside the original nations, it would have to be Western Europe. In fact, some aspects of European culture were even more advanced down this line, especially the film industry – which was already a lot more sexually explicit on the continent than it was in Britain or the USA.

But as the sexual revolution got into full swing during the 1960s and 1970s, we see in Europe the same changes in music and media, the same declines in marriage and family formation, the same catastrophic drop-off in birthrates, the same jumps in divorce, broken homes, drug abuse and societal decay.[1] Even among the more Catholic nations of Southern Europe the picture was the same – though often slightly delayed.

In Italy the birthrate did not actually fall below the "replacement" rate until 1977 – though it had been trending downward since the mid-1960s. Spain managed to stay above replacement all the way to 1981, but quickly succumbed after that. Portugal suffered the same fate the following year – 1982.[2]

Today, these nations are among the worst demographic basket-cases on earth. Their birthrates have been so low for so long that deaths far outnumber births every year. In 2014, Italy's population actually began to shrink outright. As of this writing, that nation has already lost over a million people. And it will continue to decline year after year, into the foreseeable future. Portugal too has begun shrinking away, while Spain sits right on the edge of the abyss. [3]

These declines are so great that even large-scale immigration cannot make up the numbers. And this is the case for other European nations also. The entire region is staring down the barrel of demographic catastrophe. And as this whole thing accelerates to the downside, they will lose tens of millions of people in the years ahead. [4]

CHILDBIRTH UNDERMINED

Of course, these trends go far beyond just the Western countries. In the previous chapter we looked at the impact of the sexual revolution across the developed world. We also discussed the contraceptive revolution in science that underpinned it – and the invention of the birth-control pill. But do these events have anything to do with the epic collapse in birthrates that has occurred even in far-flung regions of the earth? Of course! You don't have to be in the West to be influenced by the West. The "new media" crosses every border. There is no question that these developments have had a profound impact in nation after nation, right around the globe.

When a study such as the Washington University one (quoted in the first chapter) gives reasons for these declines, they often say something like this: "Our findings suggest that continued trends in female educational attainment and access to contraception will hasten declines in fertility and slow population growth." [5] In other words, it is mostly down to female schooling and birth control. But they know full-well that this is not the whole story (though it is hardly politically correct to say so).

If they were being honest, what these people should be highlighting is "female education followed by a career." For that is the real game-changer. It is not simply that more females are receiving a higher education. It is that they are then expected to follow it with a working career that often takes them away from motherhood right through their prime child-bearing years.[6]

Many women these days are expected to get a university degree and then work a full-time job for the best 15 years of their life, finally popping out a couple of babies in their mid-thirties, at which time they will place their small infants in daycare and go right back to work. Sadly for many women, however, they find that getting pregnant in their thirties is not so easy. As medical experts make clear, the longer a woman waits past her twenties, the more difficult and hazardous her pregnancies are likely to be.

The American College of Obstetricians and Gynecologists states: "A woman's peak reproductive years are between the late teens and late 20s. By age 30, fertility (the ability to get pregnant) starts to decline. This decline becomes more rapid once you reach your mid-30s... Women who get pregnant later in life have a higher risk of complications... as a woman ages, the risk of having a baby with missing, damaged, or extra chromosomes increases." [7]

ATTACK ON MOTHERHOOD

As stated above, these risks and difficulties grow rapidly after the age of thirty – and especially after age 35. Thus we can see how harmful it is to push women away from motherhood right through their twenties. This is, in fact, one of the most "revolutionary" (and most damaging) aspects of the sexual revolution. The undermining of motherhood in these key childbearing years, and the constant pressure on young women to choose career over children – right through the prime of their life.

This pressure only started in the late 1960s and early 1970s. Before that, most women were expected to stay home and raise a family. That was the norm. But then came an enormous propaganda campaign to get them into the workforce. "You go girl" and "Girls can do anything," yelled the advertisements. No wonder big corporations loved the sexual revolution!

Thus the ranks of both workers and university students swelled, along with a whole fresh wave of female consumers, newly flush with cash. Prices went up, up, up, while birthrates went down, down, down. Both the age of first marriage and the age of first childbirth began to get pushed further and further back. Couples that had once got married in their early twenties and started a family right away, were now waiting until closer to thirty and putting off having children as long as possible.[8]

An entire world of possibilities seemed to open up – a consumerist utopia where you spend more and more time on yourself, and less and less time raising children. Since so many women were now in the workforce, this enabled the price of houses to go higher and higher. In most big cities in the West today, it takes two people working full-time to afford a reasonable home. In the old days it took only one.

A subtle denigration of motherhood underpinned this entire movement. It was no longer considered "enough" simply to be a great mother to one's children. Women had to have a fulfilling career or their life was considered "wasted" or stunted in some way. Career was to come first, marriage and family second. More and more women began to "play the field," and it was not uncommon for some to have dozens of sexual partners before finally settling down.[9] For all of human history such behavior had been utterly taboo. Now it was simply considered "normal."

You would think, with all this sexual liberation going on, that women's happiness would be through the roof. After all, they were now supposedly getting everything they ever wanted. A great career, lots of consumerist "toys" to play with, reams of uncommitted sex, a family only if and when they desired, etc. They had been set free from the "prison" of a family-centered life. How could they not rejoice?

But tellingly, measures of women's happiness now began a long, multi-decade slump from which they have never recovered.[10] Today, women are, on average, less happy even than men, who have experienced their own decline since the 1970s. The mental health of women has also become far more precarious, with rates of depression, suicide and anxiety far worse today than before the sexual revolution.[11]

A DYSFUNCTIONAL WASTELAND

The fact is, motherhood badly needs to be reclaimed from the revolutionaries who stole it fifty years ago. It needs to once again be seen as "enough" simply to be a great mother and homemaker. Our society has lost so much by devaluing the family and promoting consumerist materialism in its place. Having children used to be seen as a blessing. Today, kids are too often viewed as an inconvenience. We need to get back to the place where devoting oneself to motherhood and the family is not considered a "waste," but rather one of the most noble and vital callings on the planet.

The dating and marriage market in the West has likewise become utterly dysfunctional in modern times. "Hookup" culture and dating apps such as Tinder and Bumble have only made the problem worse, not better. Some call it the "dating apocalypse." No wonder marriage rates are at record lows!

All of this puts continuous downward pressure on birthrates and family formation. It is simply a vicious cycle that goes around and around until entire nations are falling apart at the seams. And then comes the endgame.

It is tragic to see today's younger generations growing up in a world of such dysfunction and uncertainty. Sexual hookups and uncommitted couplings are the norm. Marriage is a dying institution. But what few realize is that when sex is so cheap and the idea of "keeping oneself" for marriage is mocked and derided, the very bedrock of our society is under threat – and the future grows darker by the day. All history shouts this warning. Such a culture cannot and will not survive.

Deep down a lot of young people know that something is terribly wrong. They feel the ground shifting beneath their feet and they know something vital has been lost. In today's media, about the only place you can see marriage and sexual purity being promoted is in old Jane Austen novels and period dramas. No wonder these books and series have made such a huge comeback – especially among young women. There is a deep longing for the old norms to return. But alas that world is utterly gone – seemingly forever.

Never forget that when you hear songs on the radio, or see shows on TV, that promote uncommitted sex or undermine religious faith or poke fun at marriage – that they are part of a multi-decade effort that has ruined our culture and destroyed much of the fabric of our society. These themes are now so ingrained and commonplace that we hardly even notice them any more. But that is how we know they've been successful. These revolutionaries have remade the world in their own image. And the result is a moral and familial wasteland of truly epic proportions.

FERTILITY CRASH

There is one measure of birthrates that you will see again and again in this book. It is the one most favored by demographers and is, in many ways, the easiest to understand. It is known as "TFR" or Total Fertility Rate. So what does TFR actually mean? Well, it is the total number of children born to a woman in her lifetime. If a woman has three children in her whole life, then the Total Fertility Rate for that woman = 3. And if all the women in a particular country have an average of 2.5 children each, then we would say that the TFR of that country = 2.5.

Now think about this for a moment. How many children does each woman need to simply "replace" the population – or keep it stable? A lot of people would say that each female simply needs two children – one to replace the mother and one to replace the father. In theory, that should keep the population perfectly steady – neither growing nor shrinking. Just staying the same.

But what we find in practice is that developed nations need the fertility rate to be about 2.1. This is because some infants die young and there are accidents, etc. Not all children live into adulthood. So the "replacement rate" for most developed countries is around 2.1. Any lower than that and the country faces outright shrinkage at some point in the future.

If the fertility rate falls well below replacement then the danger becomes even more urgent. No country with half a brain wants it's population declining. They know they're flirting with social and economic disaster if they let the fertility rate get too low.[12]

(Please bear in mind that the replacement rate in poorer nations like Niger and Bangladesh is actually somewhat higher – because of infant mortality and child deaths. Usually it is around 2.3 or 2.4 in these cases).

Of course, when we talk about a country with fertility that is "below replacement," what we are saying is that their population is at stall speed, and in due time their economy – and their entire society – is bound to follow.[13]

LIKE THE TITANIC

It can be helpful to think of population as being a bit like the great ship *Titanic*. Because of it's vast size, change takes effect very slowly. You may see an iceberg ahead, but the steering takes effect too slowly for you to avoid it. And even after the ship has been holed it still sits stalled in the water for hours before it actually sinks.

Similarly, when a population hits the "iceberg" of sub-replacement fertility it can take years for that country to begin to sink. And when it does happen it is very slow at first. A lot of people can't understand this. They think, "The fertility rate just fell to 1.7. Why are we not shrinking away immediately?" Well, these things take time. It is a generational process that can take decades. But when it does begin to bite it is almost impossible to reverse.

Today we have many nations that have been sitting filling with "water" for decades. And now they are about to start the process of sinking beneath the waves. Think of a car driving up a slight incline. You can turn the engine off, but still the car may coast further up the rise for awhile before coming to a stop. And then, faster and faster, it begins to roll back down the hill from whence it came.

For most developed nations today, they hit sub-replacement fertility decades ago. And they think they have gotten away with it. But now comes the reckoning. The vessel has been filling with water all this time. And the moment has now come for her to begin to sink.

A COLLAPSING EUROPE

The sad fact is, there is not one nation in the whole of Europe that is actually thriving demographically. Most of them exist on a scale from "stagnating" to disastrous. The majority of them plunged below replacement around 1973 – and have remained there ever since. Today the TFR of Austria is around 1.44, the TFR of Switzerland is about 1.46, and the population of Greece is actually shrinking already.[14] Many of these countries sit right on the edge of the precipice – ready to tip over at any moment.

The nation of Germany is an important example. As most people know, this is the economic powerhouse of Europe. German banking, German engineering, German technology and the German auto industry have made the country a titan of industrial strength and know-how. Think of these well-known brands: Mercedes, BMW, Volkswagon, BASF, Nivea and Adidas. German GDP is the highest of any nation on the continent. Where Germany goes, so goes Europe.

But when it comes to demographics, Germany has been a disaster-in-waiting for so long that it is a miracle they have survived as well as they have. The country has managed it largely by being a huge export-driven powerhouse (like Japan) – but also with the skillful use of immigration to cover their shortfall of workers. Sadly for Germany, however, this model is completely unsustainable. It cannot and will not last. Today, deaths outnumber births by more than a hundred thousand per year.[15] And it only gets worse from here.

PEAKING TWICE

Germany actually has a slightly unusual history in terms of its demographics. After years and years of chronically-low birthrates, the country's population finally peaked at 82.5 million in the year 2003. By 2009 they had lost 600,000 people. And by the year 2012, deaths were outnumbering births by almost 200,000 per year.[16] Clearly something had to be done. And immigration was the only real tool available. Somehow the intake of people would have to be drastically increased.

In 2015 an unexpected opportunity arose. And Germany seized it with the grasp of a drowning man. It was the great Syrian refugee crisis. Thousands upon thousands of Middle-Eastern refugees were flooding across the Bosphorus strait into southern Europe. It was a huge humanitarian disaster. Many nations opened their arms to take in hundreds – or even thousands – of these displaced people. Germany announced it was taking in a million.

Across the world people were astounded. One million refugees! Who ever heard of such a thing? But as we have seen, Germany had her reasons. The results, however, would certainly be controversial. There was a huge political backlash, not just in Germany, but right across the continent. Taking in the dispossessed was one thing, but the sheer numbers seemed incomprehensible.

THE RESULTS

So did this dramatic gesture by Germany actually help her demographic profile? Well yes, it did – but only a little. The fertility rate ticked up from the 1.4s into the 1.5s (still well below replacement). And by 2018 the country even managed the difficult feat of topping its previous peak in population. (The peak back in 2003 had been 82.5 million. But now it crept up over 83 million for the first time).[17] This boon can only ever be temporary, however.

As the *Economist* magazine stated, a year after this grand German gesture: "Last year, as the magnitude of the refugee inflows became clear, Vítor Constâncio, a vice-president of the European Central Bank, said that immigrants could stop Europe from committing "demographic suicide". But migrants are no demographic panacea."

The article continued: "The scale of immigration needed to compensate for Europe's rising age profile is politically implausible. Germany's Federal Statistics Office recently calculated that the country would need to accept 470,000 working-age migrants a year to offset its demographic decline. And the migrants would have to keep coming, because they age, too, and their fertility rates tend quickly to converge with those of the native population."[18]

There it is. 470,000 immigrants needed every year – just in Germany alone. Year in and year out. A never-ending stream. That is what it would take simply to stabilize the population. And as we have seen, such a number is politically untenable. Such an inflow would create enormous problems just by itself.

Problems and pressures that could topple governments – and lead to the rise of anti-immigrant extremists.

Already we see this happening – even though Germany is nowhere near that level of constant immigration. Such is the dilemma that the country now finds itself in. Stuck between a rock and a hard place. Desperately in need of greater inflows – and yet not daring to act lest the political fallout become too extreme.

And dozens of other countries face exactly the same predicament.

UNAVOIDABLE

So what of Germany's future? Well, even after all this immigration, the German government itself now predicts that sometime after 2024 the population will begin to shrink again. For a certainty, they believe, the working-age population will fall by between 4 and 6 million by the year 2035. And by 2060 they project that the country's overall population may be as low as 74 million – and shrinking every year.[19]

The big question is – at what point does Germany's economy go into a tailspin? And how will all these immigrants react when that happens? Will they stay in a recession-ridden Germany – as the jobs and prosperity shrink away – or will they leave for greener pastures? It must be remembered that the EU has open borders – and there is nothing to stop them leaving.

Either way, the country is in deep trouble. And this is Europe's leading economy we are talking about. A major engine of

European prosperity. What happens to the rest of the continent when Germany falls away? In fact, what happens to the entire planet?

IS EUROPE DYING?

The short answer to this question is, "Yes." But different parts of Europe are dying at different rates. Some commentators point to France and Norway as examples of countries that are doing well in this regard. And it is true that they are doing better than Germany. But both these nations are below replacement – and have been since the 1970s. France has averaged a TFR of about 1.9 over the last 30 years, while Norway has averaged about 1.8.[20]

Like all of Europe, these countries rely on constant immigration to make up the shortfall. And these are the best of the bunch. In fact, they are way out in front of the vast bulk of European nations. (The average TFR for Europe as a whole is roughly 1.53).

Generally speaking, the birthrates on the continent tend to get better the further north you go – up in the Scandinavian countries in particular. But the reckoning day is approaching fast. Across Europe, working populations are turning down, schools are closing, towns and villages are emptying out. For a lot of countries, it is only a matter of time before the endgame kicks in. This vital region that once ruled half the globe is facing a gloomy future.

THE MUSLIM QUESTION

But what about the Islamic immigrants, you ask? Aren't the Muslims going to take over as the Europeans die off? Well, this is certainly a popular myth that has been circulating for some time. But as the *Economist* magazine states: "Migrants... age, too, and their fertility rates tend quickly to converge with those of the native population." [21]

Yes – exactly. Their fertility rates converge. In nation after nation this has been found to be the case. As demography experts Darrell Bricker and John Ibbitson state: "Immigrants—including Muslim immigrants—swiftly adopt the native country's fertility rate. New arrivals only take one generation to adapt to the fundamental reality of urban, twenty-first-century life: children are something to be treasured in small quantities." [22] And as the *Economist* magazine adds: "This happens fast: some studies suggest that a girl who migrates before her teens behaves much like a native." [23]

There you have it. Young people tend to adopt the norms of the country they grow up in – and their birthrates soon converge. Which means that Muslims are unlikely to be taking over anytime soon. What is far more likely is that Europe will simply empty out.

As you might expect in such a scenario, the countryside is the first to go. Entire villages become abandoned. In many places this is already happening. (Italy and East Germany, for example). It is the rural towns and hamlets that suffer the downturn first.

The big cities will be the last ones standing. In fact, if the twentieth century tells us anything, it is that humans will continue to crowd into cities right to the very end. That big-city lifestyle is impossible to resist. People will go where the jobs are – where the money is – where the toys are. Even if the lifestyle leads to demographic decline, it is simply too delectable to resist.

AN ELDERLY AVALANCHE

One of the most obvious results of all this is an absolute tidal-wave of old people. It will be the age of the elderly.[24] I don't think the current generation can even begin to imagine what the graying of an entire population looks like. How will the medical system cope? How will the social welfare system survive? How high will the taxes need to go? The numbers will be staggering.

Sadly, there are many nations that simply will not be able to afford the elderly wave that is coming.[25] Even rich countries will struggle, but many medium and undeveloped economies will end up with a nightmare on their hands. What to do with an avalanche of the old? Many will have health problems or will not own their own homes. Many will have no retirement savings to speak of. Others will have very few family members to help. What on earth will happen to these people?

The word "crisis" doesn't even begin to describe what it will be like to be old and poor in an aging, crumbling society. Many elderly will perish alone and uncared-for. The old-age homes will be overflowing and often neglected. If you are rich, you will likely do OK. If you are poor or your country cannot cope – then you are in trouble.

Few of us have lived in such an aged society before. But we are about to find out exactly what it's like. The tsunami is almost upon us. A retirement crisis like no other.

ECONOMIC FALLOUT

So what will happen to the world economy when we lose Europe? (For lose her we will). When that continent sinks into something like a permanent slump – a never-ending recession – what effect will it have?

You may think I'm being hyperbolic here, but just look at the data. As we noted earlier, the fate of Germany is basically the fate of the entire continent. Europe cannot and will not survive the eclipse of its most vital economy. The whole world is in for a wild ride as Europe comes unglued. And frankly, there seems to be no way out.

From the statistics available, I am convinced this will not even take forty years. Within just thirty years, I believe, we will see Europe enter an economic death-spiral from which she will never recover. And as everyone knows, Europe has one of the highest GDPs on earth – with probably the largest consumer-base on the planet. In fact, the consumers of Europe far outnumber even those of America. What happens, then, when she falls?

CHAPTER FIVE

AN EMPTY PLANET?

In 2019, two respected Canadian authors, Darrell Bricker and John Ibbitson, released a book called *Empty Planet: The Shock of Global Population Decline*. The pair had literally traveled the globe, interviewing demographers and others in an effort to get to the bottom of where earth's population is headed.

Their conclusions after conducting all this research were pretty stark: "The great defining event of the twenty-first century—one of the great defining events in human history—will occur in three decades, give or take, when the global population starts to decline. Once that decline begins, it will never end," they wrote.

The pair continued: "We do not face the challenge of a population bomb but of a population bust—a relentless, generation-after-generation culling of the human herd. Nothing like this has ever happened before. If you find this news shocking, that's not surprising.

"The United Nations forecasts that our population will grow from seven billion to eleven billion in this century before leveling off after 2100. But an increasing number of demographers around the world believe the UN estimates are far too high. More likely, they say, the planet's population will peak at around nine billion sometime between 2040 and 2060, and then start to decline."[1]

Later in the book, Bricker and Ibbitson make the following eye-opening statement: "The human herd has been culled in the past by famine or plague. This time, we are culling ourselves; we are choosing to become fewer. Will our choice be permanent? The answer is: probably yes."[2]

FINANCIAL FAILURE FIRST

From the days of Adam Smith and *The Wealth of Nations,* it has been recognized by most economists that a declining population is likely to cause financial fallout that can become pretty severe. The reasons for this are obvious.

Speaking of the decline of large families and the emergence of smaller ones, the authors of *Empty Planet* write: "Small families are hard on an economy. As we've seen, they reduce the number of consumers available to purchase goods. They reduce the number of taxpayers available to fund social programs. They reduce the number of young, innovative minds... The influence of children, or the lack of them, on a nation's economy is profound."[3]

Please remember that for the richer, more developed nations, peak population (and therefore "peak economy") arrives much earlier than the actual global peak. As we know, for many developed countries like Portugal, Italy and Greece this peak has already occurred. For others, their peak will come in the 2020s to 2040s. And, as Bricker and Ibbitson put it, "Once that decline begins, it will never end." But why is this? Why is a recovery so unlikely?

Well, once a nation has spent decades below replacement, the data shows that a sudden population boom out of nowhere is almost impossible. This is because the number of women of childbearing age also declines away. The pool of potential mothers becomes smaller and smaller. And before long it literally reaches the point of no return.

So is there evidence that a declining population could actually crash the economy? Many economists would say a resounding "Yes." There is abundant evidence for this. [4]

AN IMPORTANT ANALOGY

Tell me – have you ever visited a ghost town or a ghost village? They are often fun to visit in a spooky kind of way. But then the question arises: Why were they abandoned? What would cause all the people in a once-thriving town to slowly trickle away?

There are some important insights to be gained about the effects of population decline in such a scenario. So let us invent for ourselves an imaginary town of 100 people. We will call it *Smalltown*. And we will say that at the start, the population of the town is declining by exactly one person per year. Not a very drastic decline. But the effects will be notable none-the-less.

Our village of *Smalltown* has three shops – the butcher, the general store and the Post Office. How long do you think these shops will survive as the population decline goes on?

So – let us begin the process. In the first year the population goes down by one. Nobody pays a lot of attention. The same goes for the second and third years. Not much notice is paid.

But around the fifth year, suddenly people look up and take stock of the fact that the town has lost 5 percent of its population. (It has gone from 100 down to 95). This begins to become noticeable – and an air of disquiet begins to be felt. The butcher is complaining to his wife that two of his best customers have gone – and revenue is down.

WHO PANICS FIRST?

By the ten-year mark the disquiet has turned into a kind of ambient alarm. 10 percent of the population has disappeared. The butcher is still making money from his store – but less and less every year. He knows that if this carries on, soon he will be in trouble. Some of the townsfolk are getting worried about their house values. Should they get out now, while it is still possible to sell?

At the fifteen-year mark – this is where things accelerate. Not only has the town declined by fifteen, but the butcher has also shut up shop and left – along with his wife and daughter. His store stands empty with a faded "For Lease" sign like an ugly missing tooth in the center of town. Two of the most prominent families have also left – sensing the collapse to come. The school is down to eighteen children – and there is talk of busing the kids to the next town and closing the school for good. *Smalltown* now declines to 67 people. And still the descent goes on.

Ten years later we reach the 25-year mark and things are really on the skids. The school has closed and most of the remaining families have left. The Post Office has shuttered and moved it's operations into the general store. Half the houses around town are boarded up. Everyone knows that *Smalltown* is dying. It is only a matter of time.

And so it goes on, until the general store itself closes and only the elderly remain...

IS THIS SCENARIO REALISTIC?

Sure it's realistic. A little oversimplified, perhaps. But a very similar scenario has played out over and over in lost villages around the world. And it actually gives us some idea of why it is so difficult for an economy to survive a declining population. But aren't nation-sized economies more complex than village-sized ones? Of course they are – but the same principles apply.

As a nation you can do all kinds of things to paper over the cracks and delay the inevitable. You can borrow huge sums of money. You can build apartments and roads and bridges to nowhere – all in an effort to stimulate the economy. You can print barrow-loads of cash – or issue government bonds and buy them back yourself. There are any number of financial tricks you can get up to. But nothing will make up for a declining population – nothing.

After all, there is one thing that a government can never manufacture. They cannot make children. It is up to people to do that. And this is what is no longer happening.

And thus governments play their one remaining card: Immigration. Since not enough babies are being made locally, they try to import their way out of trouble. But as we saw in the previous chapter, this solution is unsustainable in the long run. Eventually the shortfall simply becomes too great. The sheer numbers that are required start to become overwhelming. (We are talking millions upon millions – staggering numbers). Immigration by itself can never be the panacea to solve this problem.

And so the endgame arrives.

WHICH COMPANIES WILL DIE?

In 2017, one of America's largest toy retailers, *Toys 'R' Us,* filed for bankruptcy. In its annual report, the company gave some surprising reasons for why sales had been declining: "Most of our end-customers are newborns and children and, as a result, our revenue are dependent on the birthrates in countries where we operate. In recent years, many countries' birthrates have dropped or stagnated as their population ages... Significant decline in the number of newborns and children in these countries could have a material adverse effect on our operating results."[5]

Many people questioned whether birthrates could actually have the kind of impact that the company was claiming. However, the Washington Post in an article entitled, "Toys R Us' baby problem is everybody's baby problem," made the following statement: "Toys R Us... also operates the Babies R Us stores. The company claims in its annual report that its income is linked to birthrates, and they appear to be right. The change in the number of children born in the previous 12 years (and thus sitting right within the Toys R Us demographic) tracks closely with the company's changing annual revenue."

The article continued: "That's why the company's demise should worry the rest of us. Toys R Us focuses on kids, so it's feeling the crunch from declining birthrates long before the rest of the economy. But it's just a matter of time before the trends that toppled the troubled toymaker put the squeeze on businesses that cater to consumers of all ages... In the end, Toys R Us will just have been the first of many businesses of all descriptions facing the same hard demographic truth: Economic growth is extremely difficult without population growth." [6]

There it is. "Economic growth is extremely difficult without population growth." A true saying that is about to catch many companies and businesses sadly unawares.

CHAPTER SIX

THE EASTERN DEATH SPIRAL

In February 2022 Russia invaded Ukraine – an event that set off huge ripples around the globe. But what a lot of people don't realize is that both Russia and Ukraine had been in terrible demographic trouble for decades prior to the war. Could this demographic crisis have affected Russia's decision to invade? Hard to say. But it certainly must have influenced Putin's thinking as he weighed up his course of action – and whether time was on his side.

Of course, in earlier decades Russia had been head of the much-feared Soviet communist empire – an empire that rivaled the United States for nuclear weapons, armies and instruments of mass destruction. From the 1940s to the 1980s, the threat of the Soviet Union and the cold war kept westerners up at night. The thought of seven thousand Russian warheads pointed at the non-communist nations was enough to send chills down many a spine.

But then in 1989, it all came tumbling down. And with the Soviet Union's demise, a dark period began for a lot of these ex-communist nations – a period that most of them still have not recovered from. In fact, it looks very much like the majority will never recover – including Russia itself.

And Ukraine was no exception.

UKRAINE – BEFORE THE WAR

In the days of the USSR, Ukraine was, of course, a close Russian ally – and one of the largest nations inside the Soviet bloc. At her peak in 1993, Ukraine had a population of just over 52 million, and a fertility rate that had been hovering around replacement for several decades.[1]

However, after the fall of the Soviet Union around 1989-1990, Ukraine's doors blew open and people began to leave – first in their thousands – then in their millions. And not only that, but the TFR fell off a cliff – spiraling downward every year until 2001, when it reached a record low of 1.09. That's right. A fertility rate so bad that it was virtually a European record.

But the difference with Ukraine was that she didn't have much immigration to help make up the shortfall. In fact, she had the opposite problem. Thousands were still leaving. By 2018, Ukraine's population had collapsed from 52 million down to 42 million – and still falling. 10 million citizens lost.[2]

EXTINCTION WATCH

Thus, even before the war, deaths outnumbered births in Ukraine by more than 200 thousand per year. The nation's TFR had semi-stabilized around 1.4. But frankly, Ukraine was in such serious demographic trouble that it was hard to see any upside. For many of these eastern states, the collapse of the Soviet empire had become virtually an "extinction level" event. And sadly, it seemed there was never going to be a recovery.

All of this was the state of things before conflict even broke out. And of course, since the invasion, millions more refugees have been fleeing Ukraine at an unprecedented rate. No matter the outcome of the war, most of these people will never return. Ukraine lies in tatters, and her population crisis can only get worse from here. Speaking in purely demographic terms it is a double catastrophe for the region – giving people even more incentive to get out now while the going is good.

REST OF THE EAST

If you ever look up a chart of the fastest-shrinking nations on earth, a large number of them will be found in the former Soviet bloc. The region has been under extinction watch for years, and the Ukraine war is only making things worse.

In 2019, one eastern European news outlet reported: "The populations of Central, Eastern, and Southeastern European (CESEE) countries are expected to decrease significantly over the next 30 years, driven by low or negative net birth rates and outward migration... Bulgaria, Latvia, Poland, and Ukraine are projected to experience the worst labour force declines, more than 30 per cent, by 2050."[3]

Sadly, these nations are literally in a death-spiral from which there is no return. Even without the war, every population projection is negative. Perhaps in 300 years some new group may re-settle the region once again. But for now it looks to be all over for these sinking eastern states.

That is how serious demographic decline can become. And Russia, the leading power in the region, has not been doing too much better.

PORTENTS OF RUSSIAN COLLAPSE

Earlier in this chapter we raised the question of whether the disastrous demographics of Russia might have had some bearing on her decision to invade Ukraine. It is an important question. Most demographers had always assumed that the aging of a military power would likely cause it to become less aggressive and more peaceful. But what if it added a sense of urgency and desperation instead? What if it caused the military power to conclude that unless it acted soon, it may eventually lose the ability to act at all? Such questions are not only faced by Russia, but also other great powers today – notably China.

As we have seen, Russia has been in deep demographic trouble since the Soviet collapse – similar to Ukraine, but not quite as severe. Bad enough to sink her as a major power, though? Yes – most demographers would say so. And nothing she has tried has ever been enough to stop the rot.

As the *Moscow Times* reported in 2019: "Top Russian Official Warns of 'Catastrophic' Population Loss... Russia's population numbers are declining "catastrophically" with several regions vastly underestimating their death rates, a top government official has said."[4]

Just a month earlier, in June 2019, the same newspaper had reported: "UN Predicts Russia's Population Could Halve By 2100... Russia's population could decrease by half by the end of this century, a new United Nations demographic report has said... In 2018, Russia's population declined for the first time in a decade to 146.8 million, while its migration numbers hit a record low."[5]

Of course, it should be remembered that Russia is by far the largest nation physically on planet earth. Even without her smaller satellites, the land area of Russia alone is more than 17 million square kilometers. She covers more than one-eighth of the inhabited land in the entire world. Little wonder then, that Russia was able to establish herself as head of a vast and powerful empire.

And she is still powerful to this day. But not for too many decades longer – if demographics have their say.

DEATH BY VODKA

Unlike Ukraine, Russia has demonstrated the power to draw in large numbers of migrants from other nations. And in 2006 she launched a special program aimed at attracting ethnic Russians from all the countries round about.

Generally, this policy has been something of a success. However, like other immigrant solutions around the world, the benefits are largely temporary. The long-term prospects for Russia are still bleak – especially since its birthrate has been well below replacement now for roughly 30 years.[6]

Of course, we should also factor in the striking number of alcohol-related deaths that Russia suffers every year – especially among males. Russian men have literally been drinking themselves to death for decades – particularly since the fall of the USSR. What this has meant is that the country has one of the highest overall death-rates on the planet.[7]

As *Radio Free Europe* reported: "The past 10 years have seen the longest anti-alcohol campaign in Russian history, with measures including a ban on advertising hard alcohol and plans to halve overall consumption."

The piece continued: "From the mid-1960s to the late 1980s, the Russian population rose steadily, but the collapse of the Soviet Union ushered in a population crisis compounded by wage arrears, mass unemployment, and alcohol abuse... Demography experts predict a steady overall population decline in the years to come."[8]

WANTING TO LEAVE

Meanwhile, large-scale immigration from nearby countries has been largely drying up. And for Russia, just like Germany, collapse is inevitable without this constant, high immigration.

Even before the war, the *Financial Observer* reported: "As if the falling numbers in immigration rates to Russia wasn't bad enough... another survey shows a record amount of Russians wanting to leave their country of birth... Since 2014, the percentage of working-age Russian citizens who say they would like to move abroad has at least tripled."[9]

No doubt these numbers are even higher now. But either way, it has been clear for some time that in the long run, Russia is a demographic disaster-zone – just like Italy and Germany. And please note how important each of these nations is to their respective regions. In each case they are a leading economic power – crucial to keeping their area afloat. (In this case, the entire Russian Federation and beyond).

There is no question that what we are facing here is a synchronized international collapse – both economically and demographically. And unlike any other slump in history, this one has no ending. We cannot foresee a time when the spiral will stop. It will simply go on and on and on. This is not like the Great Depression of the 1930s or the Great Recession of the 2000s. This thing is on an entirely different scale altogether.

To repeat the ominous forecast of the book *Empty Planet:* "We do not face the challenge of a population bomb but of a population bust—a relentless, generation-after-generation culling of the human herd. Nothing like this has ever happened before." [10]

NUCLEAR FALLOUT

At the height of its power in the cold war years, the Soviet Union boasted an arsenal of about 45 thousand nuclear warheads. Even today, statistics tell us that the Russian Federation possesses 7,850 total nuclear weapons, of which 1,600 are strategically operational. The USA and Russia still control 90 percent of all nuclear warheads on earth between the two of them – even to this day.[11]

So what happens when a great nuclear superpower not only falls into decline, but slowly begins to shrink away to nothing? What happens to the world when that occurs? Does the balance of power completely fall apart? Do other nations such as China begin to make a move on vast areas of Russia's hinterland – since virtually no-one is there to stop them? Does the disintegration and fall of Russia make the world a more dangerous or less dangerous place?

We are about to find out what happens when great powers and entire regions collapse – not just in one part of the world – but all over the globe at once. What is coming is utterly unprecedented. It has never been seen before. Not in the years of the Black Death. Not in the thirty-years' war. Not at any time. A global, coordinated collapse of unprecedented size and scope.

EMPIRE OF NO-ONE

In 2019, in an article headlined, "The emptying East of Europe," *Mercatornet* reported: "From the Baltic to the Balkans, through Poland, Hungary and Bulgaria, there is a half continent that is ageing, not reproducing itself and seeing its remaining young leave for jobs elsewhere. The numbers are gloomy. Within Eastern Europe are the two fastest shrinking populations in the world." [12]

That same year, *Balkan Insight* chimed in with this eye-catching report: "Bye-Bye Balkans: A Region in Critical Demographic Decline... Former communist countries in Southeast Europe face catastrophic depopulation, with far-reaching social and political consequences. Young people are leaving. Fertility rates have collapsed. Societies are ageing. And though hundreds of thousands of refugees and migrants have tramped through much of the region, few want to stay."

The report went on: "From Greece to Poland, almost all Eastern, Central and Southeast European countries are wrestling with the same problems... The demographic future of the Balkans and this half of Europe, afflicted by emigration and chronic low birth rates, is dramatic. That is one of the reasons why what is happening today is so different from the past."[13]

Indeed – it is different. An entire continent shrinking away. Over the next 100 years, expect the whole place to empty out – with just a few large cities like Moscow left standing economically.

As we have seen, projections call for Russia's population to halve by 2100 – and for the former Soviet bloc as a whole to decline by two-thirds. It will be one of the worst demographic collapses ever recorded. The physical scale is enormous – encompassing the greatest landmass on earth (and more).

Such is the nature of the demographic calamity that lies directly ahead. It is the entire developed and semi-developed world that will be affected – not just the few areas we have discussed. This is to be the farthest-reaching "bust" our civilization has ever seen. And the most severe phase of it is only now getting underway.

CHAPTER SEVEN

JAPAN'S EPIC FALL

Japan is a tremendously rich country. Which is fortunate, because it is also in tremendous trouble. In an earlier chapter, I wrote that we can expect Japan's population to collapse from 125 million all the way down to 40 million over the next 100 years. Sadly, this is a very realistic probability. In fact, it may even be on the conservative side.[1]

In 2017 a government-affiliated research institute announced that Japan's population is expected to plunge to 88 million by 2065, marking a roughly 30 percent fall from the 2015 level. Yes – you read that right. One-third of the population gone in the space of 50 years. And these are Japanese government figures![2]

Around the globe, for years now, Japan has become known as the poster-child for demographic decline – which is alarming, because Japan is also the third-largest economy on the planet. Just think of all the top technology and auto companies that have emerged from that nation: Toyota, Nissan, Sony, Hitachi, Nintendo, Honda, Mitsubishi. The list goes on.

So what happened to Japan to turn this once-thriving economic juggernaut into a troubled, stagnating struggler? Well, financially Japan's economy had been forging ahead so powerfully by the late 1980s that two enormous bubbles formed in her stock market and her real-estate market. And finally those bubbles burst.

In December 1989, Japan's Nikkei stock index hit an all-time high of 38,916, and then began a stunning 80% crash – to a low of 7,831 more than a decade later. But of even greater concern was the fact that they never seemed to actually recover from this crash – even after 30 years. The 1990s became known as the "lost decade" in Japan – but frankly, it never truly ended.[3]

As Jim Rickards commented in *Business Insider:* "Today, a full 25 years after the bubble burst in Japan, that country continues to struggle with deflation, zero interest rates, weak banks, adverse demographics, and periodic bouts of negative growth. Japan has endured a 26-year depression, and there is no end in sight."[4]

Meanwhile, it is obvious to many that it was Japan's demography that had a huge role to play in these economic calamities.

DEMOGRAPHIC TIPPING-POINT

Like a lot of developed countries, around 1974 Japan hit sub-replacement fertility and then simply stayed there – with virtually every year worse than the last. By 1997 the TFR had sunk below 1.4 – a level that continued for much of the following two decades. Around 2007 Japan's population actually began to shrink – slowly at first – and then faster and faster. Today, Japan loses literally hundreds of thousands of people every year. And it is getting worse. It won't be long before they are losing close to a million people per annum.[5]

This is simply because so many more people are dying than are being born. But remember – Japan is only the first in a long line of nations in Asia that will suffer a similar fate.

As we have discussed before, it is very hard to grow your economy when your population is shrinking away. And one very notable factor in Japan's downfall is what is called the Working-Age Population. This is the number of people who are roughly 15–65 years old. For Japan this number peaked in 1995. And it has declined every year since then.[6]

So why is this important? Well, this is your smoking gun right here. When a country begins to lose its working-age people, what it is losing is its tax base and its consumer base. The earners are retiring. And so every year the number of taxpayers goes down. And retired people do not splurge endlessly on consumer goods either. They become much more careful with their money. This is exactly what has been happening in Japan since 1995.

Thus it is not surprising they are in an economic slump – from which there is no escape.

WHAT ABOUT IMMIGRATION?

Unfortunately, Japan has never been a culture that welcomes immigrants. Even in recent years, with a demographic crisis hanging over their heads, the people seem to have little stomach for importing newcomers. In fact, every time the government goes to implement large-scale immigration they tend to get knocked back. Most of Japan's leaders know they need it. But the political will simply isn't there. And so the shrinkage continues.

But let's be honest. There are no last-minute fixes for the kind of mess that Japan now finds itself in. Trying to bring about an inrush of immigrants at this late hour would simply be too little, too late.

Of course, one of the most obvious results of a shrinking population is the closure of schools. In 2018 the *Financial Times* said this about Japan: "In 2016, there were about 2,300 fewer kindergartens than seven years earlier as the number of pupils dropped by 18 per cent. Nearly 2,000 primary schools have been shut over the same period."[7]

In other words, over just a seven-year time frame, Japan was forced to close 2,300 kindergartens and 2,000 schools. And of course, this is only the beginning.

A STRIKING CHANGE

In previous chapters we looked at the sexual revolution and its effect on the Western world. In Japan's case, while it was certainly influenced by this revolution, the country was not a full participant in it from the start. The youth of Japan did develop an appetite for certain genres of Western rock music and entertainment, however. And the sexual side of things came into play more and more. But the country seemed to filter these influences through a uniquely Asian lens.

As the *New York Times* noted in 2019: "Japanese women are increasingly opting out of marriage altogether, focusing on their work and newfound freedoms, but also alarming politicians preoccupied with trying to reverse Japan's declining population."

The article continued: "The change is so striking that a growing number of businesses now cater to singles, and to single women in particular. There are single karaoke salons featuring women-only zones, restaurants designed for solo diners, and apartment complexes that target women looking to buy or rent homes on their own. Travel companies book tours for single women, and photo studios offer sessions in which women can don wedding dresses and pose for solo bridal portraits."[8]

According to the Japanese government, in 2018 both marriage rates and birthrates fell to the lowest level since the end of World War II. In the case of births it was the lowest level since at least 1899 – when record-keeping began.[9]

Kumiko Nemoto, a professor of sociology, commented that Japan's consumption-oriented culture means that single women with careers and money have a "wide range of activities and emotional outlets that their mothers or grandmothers did not." And, notably, Japanese women no longer feel the need of husbands to ensure their economic security.[10]

FAMOUS FOR THE WRONG REASONS

Due to its collapsing birthrate, Japan has received a good deal of attention from media around the world. Often they are treated like something of an "anomaly" – as though other countries are immune from the same social sicknesses that have overtaken Japan. Laughing references are made to the fact that adult diapers now outsell baby diapers – and that wild animals now threaten some of the locals in parts of Japan that are losing population. In 2013 the BBC even aired a documentary entitled, *No Sex Please – We're Japanese.*[11]

But what the media don't seem to realize is that when they look at Japan, they are simply looking at themselves 25 years into the future. Almost all the same trends are there – right across the developed world. Admittedly, though, Japan does seem to take things to unusual extremes. (The fad of single Japanese women "marrying themselves," for example).

However, underneath it all, the similarities are too obvious to deny. We ought to be worrying about ourselves – not just Japan. The phrase, "canary in the coalmine" certainly comes to mind.

RISE OF THE 'GRASS-EATERS'

In 2006 Japanese columnist Maki Fukasawa coined the term "Herbivore men" or Grass-eaters to describe men who have no interest in getting married or finding a girlfriend. This is a huge problem in Japan. The term *Herbivore* is also used to describe young men who have lost their "manliness." Many of these young males lock themselves away in their rooms – living in a virtual world on their computers. They say they are not interested in money or girlfriends – or living a "normal" life.[12]

Others can be found, peacocking and p the center of town. As the UK's *Indepen* "In Japan some call them herbivores, a they come out to graze: a perfume masculinity. Groomed and primped, hair perfection and bodies wrapped in tight habitat is the crowded city where they live... They spend almost as much on cosmetics and clothes as women."

The newspaper noted that Grass-eaters are "uncompetitive and uncommitted to work, a symptom of their epic disillusionment with Japan's troubled economy... Millions remain at home as "parasite singles", meaning they live with, and off, their parents. The pressing need to find a partner has been alleviated by the ubiquity of porn, sex toys and virtual sex on bedroom computers." [13]

SURPRISING NUMBERS

As Katsuhiko Kokobun, the owner of a fashionable Tokyo hair salon, told NPR: "It's not so much that men are becoming more like women. It's that the concept of masculinity is changing." Over the years, he said, greater numbers of men had been coming into his salon – men whom he described as "more modest, less demanding, kind of passive; they accept what they're told." He noticed that these men were wanting more and more traditionally-female treatments. "We do have eyebrow plucking and facials for men," he said. "Eyebrow plucking is very popular among high school boys." [14]

In the same article, NPR noted that: "Multiple recent surveys suggest that about 60 percent of young Japanese men — in early 30s — identify themselves as herbivores." ...eys put the number even higher.[15]

...er way, this means that literally hundreds of thousands of young Japanese men are displaying these 'Grass-eater' tendencies in one way or another. And needless to say, none of it is doing the country's birthrate any good.

A WORSENING SPIRAL

For years the government of Japan has tried all kinds of remedies to get the birthrate climbing again. They have tried reforming the tax code and granting couples more parental leave. They have tried giving out money for each extra child. But most radical of all, the government has even been known to sponsor "speed-dating" events in various parts of the country. Sadly, none of this seems to be making the slightest bit of difference.[16]

Meanwhile, for those under forty, Japan has virtually the worst suicide rate in the developed world (though South Korea usually beats them in suicides overall). In fact, in Japan, suicide is the number one cause of death for people in that sub-40 age group. And like most countries today, these statistics are far more severe among males.

Government figures show that more than 20,000 people kill themselves in Japan every year – which is about three times the rate in a country like the UK, for instance.[17] A terrible problem for a nation that is in the grip of a demographic crisis.

LIFE IN A SHRINKING SOCIETY

Despite all this gloom and doom, the fact is that Japan's capital Tokyo is still the world's largest city – with a population of 38 million. So do people in that city even notice that the population is shrinking away around the edges? No – they don't. And that's half the problem.

In the center of Tokyo, life is as busy as ever. The streets are still crowded. The subways are still full of people. At night the neon dance of a hundred brightly-lit signs still dominates the heart of the city. Nothing has really changed – and in fact you would never know that a demographic crisis is gripping the country. People are everywhere. Great seas of people. Vast swathes of humanity – everywhere you look. The overcrowding seems impossible to escape.

And the fact is, central Tokyo will still feel that way even after Japan has lost half its population. It is one of the great ironies of this whole business. Humans will still continue to crowd into cities – and will continue to live that hectic city lifestyle – all the way down. No doubt most Japanese will still be doing so when the population plunges below 50 million – and still falling.

By then Tokyo will likely have less than 20 million inhabitants – but it will still feel crowded in the center of town. Very likely they will simply demolish buildings, shut down some of the subways, and carry right on.

In many of its smaller cities and regions, Japan is already feeling the effects of this shrinkage that is underway. In late 2018 the government announced that more than 13 percent of all homes in the country were now unoccupied or abandoned.[18]

In some towns they are literally giving away houses for free. A CNN report stated in 2019: "As young people leave rural areas for city jobs, Japan's countryside has become haunted by deserted "ghost" houses, known as "akiya." It's predicted that by 2040, nearly 900 towns and villages across Japan will face a risk of extinction... In that context, giving away property is a bid for survival." [19]

And as the *Japan Times* reported: "Even Tokyo, which enjoys an influx of young people from across the country, expects to see the tide change after 2025, according to a forecast released by the Tokyo Metropolitan Government." [20]

The forecast states that the population of Tokyo is expected to fall 13 percent between the years 2025 and 2060. So even Tokyo – the largest city on earth – is actually about to start shrinking. (Though of course, that city will still do better than the rest of the country – due to the constant influx of young Japanese).

As you can see, it's hard to look upon Japan as anything other than a demographic disaster zone. If there is a race to the bottom, they are leading the pack. But is there any chance that the population might stabilize at some point? Sadly, the probability of this is low – especially in the next 100 years – and probably much longer. The pool of young women of childbearing age has already been shrinking for too long – so things will likely get worse over time, rather than better. As the authors of *Empty Planet* so aptly told us, "Once that decline begins, it will never end."

The third-largest economy on earth has entered its 'freefall' phase.

CHAPTER EIGHT

THE MOUSE UTOPIA EXPERIMENTS

In 1947, a scientist from Johns Hopkins University named John B. Calhoun began a series of population experiments that would later become famous around the world. In the first experiment, Calhoun built a huge quarter-acre outdoor pen which he called a "rat city," and which he seeded with five pregnant female rats. He wanted to study the effects of overcrowding.

Calhoun calculated that the enclosure could house as many as 5000 rats. Instead, the population leveled off at 150, and throughout the two years that Calhoun kept watch, never exceeded 200. The scientist was bewildered. A population of only 150 seemed pretty low. What had gone wrong?[1]

From 1954 onward, Calhoun was employed by the U.S. National Institute of Mental Health. He repeated the overcrowding experiment in specially constructed "rodent megacities" – room-sized pens which could be viewed from above. Once again he provided his populations with constant food, bedding and shelter. With no predators and with exposure to disease kept at a minimum, Calhoun described each enclosure as a "rat utopia" or a "mouse paradise." He went to great lengths to make them exceedingly safe and well-provisioned.

What Calhoun was trying to do was to find a link between the behavior of these small mammals and that of larger mammals like humans. How would they react when their every need was met with so little effort or danger? Would it help or hurt them not to have to work for food? How would they respond to a "paradise" where everything was laid on? And what about overcrowding? Would being surrounded by other animals day-in and day-out alter their behavior?

THE SURPRISING EFFECTS

A paper released by the London School of Economics describes what happened: "With all their visible needs met, the animals bred rapidly. The only restriction Calhoun imposed on his population was of space – and as the population grew, this became increasingly problematic. As the pens heaved with animals, one of his assistants described rodent "utopia" as having become "hell"." [2]

But not all the space in these megacities was overrun. Some parts were quite sparsely populated. In fact, it was the feeding areas that tended to become crowded – and where the breakdown in the rodents' social patterns was most clearly seen. This unusual behavior got more and more extreme as time went on. And it led to disaster. The greater the boom, the more severe the bust.

The LSE paper describes what happened: "Dominant males became aggressive, some moving in groups, attacking females and the young. Mating behaviors were disrupted. Some became exclusively homosexual. Others became pansexual and hypersexual, attempting to mount any rat they encountered. Mothers neglected their infants... In certain sections of the pens, infant mortality rose as high as 96%."[3]

The endgame was not long in coming: "After day 600, the social breakdown continued and the population declined toward extinction. During this period females ceased to reproduce. Their male counterparts withdrew completely, never engaging in courtship or fighting. They ate, drank, slept, and groomed themselves – all solitary pursuits. Sleek, healthy coats and an absence of scars characterized these males. They were named "the beautiful ones"."[4]

Yes – that's right. Virtually every rodent megacity that Calhoun ever created declined all the way to zero. No matter what he tried, the results were always the same. First there was a population boom – followed by aberrant social patterns – then a population bust of colossal proportions. The numbers didn't just decline by a little. They went all the way down to extinction – accompanied by rodent behavior that became more and more extreme as time went on. Calhoun called this the "behavioral sink."

WHAT ABOUT HUMANS?

Of course, it is very tempting to look at Calhoun's results and find direct parallels to our own time. Calhoun's bands of violent males become today's inner-city street gangs, stuck in an overcrowded tenement hell. His non-reproducing females become our non-reproducing females. His primping, preening "beautiful ones" become our Herbivore men – the grass-eaters who have given up on normal "manly" life to become hermits or aesthetes – devoted to grooming the "body beautiful."

The comparisons are certainly there to make – and in Calhoun's own time they were made over and over again – not just by the media – but by academics, authorities and city-planners who were deeply concerned over what modern cities could become. A human "rodent utopia" was to be avoided at all costs. Even Calhoun himself stated: "I shall largely speak of mice, but my thoughts are on man."[5]

But is it fair to make such direct comparisons? We are speaking of rodents and human beings after all – two utterly distinct and different species. However, some of the correlations are too striking to ignore. The similarities are so startling that it would be foolish to discard them entirely. There may very well be lessons to learn from the rodent megacity and its demise.

THE LARGEST YET

In 1968, John Calhoun began his most ambitious experiment ever, naming it "Universe 25." The enclosure measured 2.7 meters square and was split into four separate interconnected pens – with 16 tunnels leading to food, water, and various burrows. Four breeding pairs of mice were introduced to this spacious enclosure and were given unlimited, easy access to food and water. This mouse city was to be very well catered-for. Of course, what Calhoun was trying to do was emulate the conditions of humans in similar environments.[6]

The only limitation the mice faced would be that of physical space. They could roam anywhere in the enclosure that they liked. But sadly, this experiment was to follow very much the same course as all the others.

The rodents spent the first 104 days getting used to their environment. Then the population began to double every 55 days, until by day 315 their numbers had reached 620. At this point, the enclosure was becoming a bit crowded in some places and the birthrate plunged to a much lower rate, about one-third of what it had been before.

As always, it was the food compartments that were becoming cramped. The big enclosure itself was not overcrowded (it was built for 3,800) but there was a real imbalance developing. Some compartments were almost empty – but the feeding halls were constantly overrun. And it was noticed that any mice born in those areas were becoming socially impaired.[7]

It was at about this point that life in the mouse paradise began to fall apart.

THE BEHAVIORAL SINK

In an excellent article on this topic, researcher Brent Swancer wrote: "From around Day 315 of the experiment, a wide variety of odd behavior started to surface among the animals." He wrote that some male mice gave up on their natural instincts and stopped trying to defend their own territory or the females that were pregnant. Instead, they became "listless wanderers tending to congregate in the center of the Universe where they spent their days mindlessly eating or fighting amongst themselves. These males were seen as the "outcasts" of the society."[8]

Some of these outcasts became passive and withdrawn – seemingly not caring if they lived or died. They didn't even defend themselves when attacked. Others became violent or aggressive – viciously attacking others of any gender – or mounting and essentially "raping" them. This behavior became ever-more widespread over time.

Swancer continues: "The female mice were not having much more luck. In the absence of any males willing to protect their nests, mothers began to become highly aggressive towards trespassers, essentially taking on the role typically reserved for the males. Unfortunately, this went into overdrive...

"Some females became unusually aggressive towards even their own offspring and would even sometimes attack and kill their own young, while others became morose hermits who refused to mate. All of this led to a quickly sinking birthrate and an infant mortality rate of over 90% in some areas of the enclosure." [9]

Swancer notes Calhoun's response to this societal collapse: "Calhoun speculated that a lack of social roles to fill combined with constant, unwanted social and physical contact" was at the root of the problem. In other words, the outcasts withdrew because they had no "work" or jobs to give them purpose – since taking risks and foraging for food were no longer needed – and the crowded conditions made things even more intolerable.

No risks to take and no work to do essentially left them unemployed and useless. Thus they gave up almost entirely on social norms and fitting in. The best phrase to describe it might be "pointless despair" – leading to violence and complete withdrawal.

THE END IS NIGH

By Day 560 of the experiment, there was almost no population growth at all. The mortality rate had reached virtually 100 percent. As Brent Swancer notes: "Amid all of this turmoil and degradation within Universe 25, there was also a new generation of mice emerging that had not ever been subjected to a normal social upbringing and showed absolutely no interest in fighting, courtship, mating, raising young, or much of anything really. Calhoun referred to this aberrant group of mice as "the beautiful ones.""

These "beautiful ones" were completely detached from normal society or behavior, and spent all their time eating, sleeping or constantly grooming and preening themselves. Thus, they had a fine, sleek, healthy appearance. Calhoun often spoke of these mice as "handsome," however, their beauty was only skin deep. They were like a vacant shell. The beautiful ones lived peacefully detached and withdrawn from the rest of society.[10]

Calhoun often referred to this drastic state of withdrawal as the "first death" – basically the death of the animal's soul, which would occur before the "second death" – or physical death of the body. "Once this "first death" was reached, the mice were no longer really mice anymore but rather empty husks merely killing time awaiting the inevitable death of their body and an end to their pointless existence. They had in a sense lost all will to live in any useful manner."[11]

Calhoun later theorized that mice were in many respects like mankind, and that "in the absence of any tension, pressure, or stress they had lost their focus and sense of purpose and identity. With an overabundance of vital resources and no need to do anything to obtain them, the need for societal roles or jobs had faded... These mice, and indeed it could be inferred human beings as well, required conditions of stress, pressure, obstacles, and a clear purpose in order to have a destiny and a desire to engage in society." [12]

THE DEATH PHASE

On day 920 of the experiment the last conception was recorded. No more mice would ever be born. Even though the enclosure could house 3,800, the population had peaked at 2,200 – far below capacity. And now only extinction lay ahead.

Most of the mice now refused to mate – or to perform any useful function whatsoever. The colony was passing into shadow. And a very ugly shadow it was.

What is most surprising to many observers is that there never came a time when the mice woke up and began to behave like mice again. Even when their numbers were dwindling away, there was never a moment when they started to behave normally or to procreate once again. They had simply ceased to be mice in the usual sense. There was no chance of recovery. They had all the food and resources they would ever need, but still the colony would sink all the way down to zero.

As Brent Swancer put it: "This was the unstoppable slide to catastrophe, the point of no return, the "behavioral sink" that Calhoun had talked about, and the mouse utopia's apocalypse came crashing down as all of these factors conspired to cause the population to start barrelling rapidly towards extinction until there were none left. Universe 25 had ceased to exist." [13]

NO SURVIVORS

Desperate to salvage something, near the end Calhoun removed a few small groups of "beautiful ones" to see if they would revert to normal behavior and start a colony elsewhere. But this was a total failure. The mice were simply too far gone. There was nothing physically wrong with them, but they were just not capable of being mice any more. There was not a single birth in any of the colonies that the scientists tried to restart.

In 1973, John Calhoun released his Universe 25 results in a paper rather ominously titled, *Death Squared: The Explosive Growth and Demise of a Mouse Population.* This received a great deal of attention in the media and academic worlds.

Of course, Calhoun's experiments were already well-known across the globe. His most famous paper on this topic had been published in Scientific American back in 1962. (That paper, *Population Density and Social Pathology,* has since been named as one of "Forty Studies that Changed Psychology" – joining publications by such figures as Freud, Pavlov, Milgram, Rorschach, and Skinner).[14]

THE TAKEAWAYS FOR HUMANS

So how much relevance do these experiments have for our own species? Do they bear any relation to what has been happening in Japan or other places? How does it truly affect people to face so few risks and dangers in obtaining their food, to have every need so easily met, and to be surrounded by crowds day-in and day-out – every month of every year? What are our modern megacities actually doing to us?

Are people changed by being housed in tiny apartments in a tower block – compared with the countryside? And what effect does modern life itself have – a life of such little effort or risk – a life where everything is "laid on" – just like a rat universe? Do the "beautiful ones" have any relevance?

Well, one thing is certainly relevant. The birthrates in our most crowded cities are alarmingly low. And this is especially true of Asia – where cities are often modeled on Japan. In fact, some of China's most modern cities actually have TFRs among the lowest on earth – well under 1.0. And similar trends have been seen in Singapore, Taiwan, South Korea and Hong Kong.

Something is happening in these cities – and perhaps every large metropolis across the planet. It is something that should ring alarm bells for all of us. Little wonder that the authors of *Empty Planet* cite "urbanization" as the leading factor in the great baby bust that is occurring worldwide. It is this modern urge to crowd into cities that they believe is having the greatest impact on birthrates around the globe.

THE APPEAL OF CITY LIFE

The fact that TFRs are always lower in cities than in the countryside is something that has been known for a very long time. And it is true across the world. Cities are simply a more expensive place to raise children. Life is faster and people are busier. Food, housing, education, childcare – all of it costs more and is harder to come by. So big-city-dwellers simply choose to have less babies.

They cannot afford the time off work, after all. They need both parents working to afford the lifestyle they came for.

Despite the stresses of urban life (and they are many), it is not hard to see why more and more of us are crowding into cities every year – in nation after nation across the globe. One word: Opportunity. Cities are where the opportunities are. Money, employment and education. If we want our family to live a comfortable modern life – with all the toys and trappings that come with it – then the city is the place to be.

People do it for their kids as much as anything else. But at what cost? The cost of our psychological health and well-being? The cost of future humanity? What exactly are we sacrificing here?

A TALE OF THREE CITIES

In *The Fate of Empires,* Sir John Glubb noted the enormous appeal of the "primary city" in any civilization that is at its peak. But today we seemingly have many primary cities around the world – into which the vast masses of humanity crowd. The appeal of the modern megacity on this kind of scale has seemingly only taken off since the dawn of the Industrial age – about 260 years ago. And over that time, several of these cities stand out as having special "leadership" qualities.

There are basically three of these leading cities that have dominated over that period. Three great cities for three distinct epochs of the industrial and technological revolution. This "city-led" transformation has greatly affected us all.

Of course, it is the age of London that emerges first. London – the first industrial megacity. The largest city on earth for a period of almost 100 years – from 1826 through to 1924. The birthplace of the steam engine, the iron foundry, the cotton mill, the sweatshop. Home to the huddled masses who crowded into the great metropolis looking for work – millions and millions of them – who put up with the most appalling conditions in hopes of a better future and a higher wage.

London was the progenitor of them all, the front-runner that many would imitate. All eyes were on her. The richest (and most smog-ridden) city on earth. London became the model that many others would follow – looking for similar success, similar influence, similar wealth. But again we have to ask – at what cost? What cost to humanity itself?

ENTER THE AMERICANS

It is not hard to guess the city that was to dominate the world stage in the next phase of industrial growth. It was, of course, New York City. For basically a century leading up to 1924, London had been the most populous city on the planet. In 1925, New York took over.

New York – the city of dreams, the city of finance, the city of immigrants – of skyscrapers and entertainment – the city of all things American.

American consumerism (Fifth Avenue), American freedom (the Statue of Liberty), American advertising (Madison

Avenue), American entertainment (Broadway), American "bigness" (the Empire State building), American finance (Wall Street). The cars, the highways, the films, the jazz (later Rock 'n' Roll and Hiphop). Coca-Cola, McDonalds, movie stars, television, Elvis Presley, Marilyn Monroe. Consumer goods and home appliances by the boatload.

An entire American lifestyle sold around the world on big and small screens everywhere. A modern lifestyle, a consumerist lifestyle – a lifestyle of constant entertainment. America set the tone for generations around the world. Nobody was immune. You could live in Timbuktu and still there was a good chance you had heard of Charlie Chaplin, Frank Sinatra, or the American Atom bomb.

Even when the next great city came to the fore, it was American music, American entertainment and American culture that would continue to dominate the airwaves of much of the world. That is how powerful these forms of "soft power" had become. America had perfected them and America would continue to "own" them all the way to the end.

THE TECHNOLOGY REVOLUTION

How appropriate it is, given all that we have been discussing, that the city to take over from New York would be the city of Tokyo, Japan. It could be said that London was the city of industrial revolution, while New York was the city of cultural "consumerist" revolution. Tokyo, by contrast, would be the city of technology. If there is one place on earth that represents the electronics watershed of the last 70 years, it is the capital of Japan.

It was in 1954 that the population of Tokyo finally overtook the population of New York. And Tokyo is still the most populous city on earth – right up to the present day.

Three giant cities – three great phases of industrial transformation – along with the huge lifestyle changes that accompanied them. We are all the children of this series of giant revolutions – which truly transformed the very core of our society.

WHAT DOES TOKYO REPRESENT?

In an earlier chapter we ran through a list of some of the most significant companies to come out of Japan. Toyota, Sony, Hitachi, Nintendo, Honda, Sharp, Panasonic. On and on we could go. And just from these names alone, we can see the outline of the revolution that Japan has played a leading role in.

What Tokyo represents is the personalization of technology. Electronics for the individual. Humans connected to gizmos. Japan often didn't invent the technology. But they refined it and mass-produced it for human consumption. Japan didn't invent gaming – but their Sony and Nintendo consoles became world-leaders. Japan didn't invent the cellphone – but they did mass-produce it and make it cheaper for everyone. And they did the same for cars. And laptops. And cameras. And televisions. And music. And video.

Everything that was electronic and connected to people – Japan was a world leader in. And this had a dramatic effect on their culture – and the culture of the entire world. Humans connected to electronics are almost an entirely new species in many ways. Our behavior changes, our motivations change, our personal relationships change. Our entire way of living and communicating is transformed.

LIFE IN A BUBBLE

Think of the invention of the Sony Walkman, for instance. (1980s equivalent of the iPod). Suddenly the planet was full of people wearing headphones and listening to music – lost in their own little world. These people were living in their own reality – a bubble made for one – oblivious to all else. Nothing like it had ever happened before. 24-hour personalized entertainment.

And the same tends to be true of all these technologies. They take us out of the real world and transport us into a virtual one. We come to live in our own little bubble – oblivious to our surroundings. We talk to our phone but not to the humans around us. Distracted. Oblivious. Absorbed. Over-stimulated. Over-entertained. We become almost a new type of human.

In certain ways this reminds me very much of the mice in Universe 25. Just like them we have everything laid on – every whim supplied. The whole world is at our fingertips. With a few taps or clicks we can watch any video, contact any person, listen to any music, find out any information we desire. It is the very essence of instant gratification.

We middle-class modern humans live in an environment where all our wants and needs are met. Risks or dangers are totally minimized. Our electronic environment makes sure of it. Every moment of the day or night we are hooked-in. We can see or experience anything we want. The great city has provided all.

I am not picking on Japan here, but this is the world that Tokyo represents. And it was Japan that experienced it first – this entire electronic, bubble-like, instant-entertainment lifestyle. So why should we be surprised when it is Japan that first exhibits the symptoms of such a life? (As I said, I am not trying to pick on one particular country. All of this was inevitable anyway. Japan is simply the most apt example to point to).

In many ways this is the world we all now live in. We are all connected. We have all become bubble-dwellers. We don't need to live in a big city any more. The big city has come to us – or at least to the device at our fingertips.

A LOST GENERATION

In 2016, U.S. demographer Nicholas Eberstadt released a book entitled, *Men Without Work: America's Invisible Crisis.* In it he wrote: "In the half century between 1965 and 2015, work rates for the American male spiraled relentlessly downward, and an ominous migration commenced: a "flight from work," in which ever-growing numbers of working-age men exited the labor force altogether. America is now home to an immense army of jobless men no longer even looking for work – more than seven million alone between the ages of twenty-five and fifty-five, the traditional prime of working life." [15]

Of course, this phenomenon is not just confined to America – or Japan. Right across the developed world there are millions of males on 'disability' or living rent-free in their parents' homes. Many play video games all hours of the day and night. They watch porn, text their friends, and live a life that is hardly any life at all. No girlfriend, no career, no future. Millions of them.

It is our technology that is enabling this. In fact, it would be virtually impossible without it.

By the standards of previous generations, this is completely abnormal behavior. And it is quite a recent phenomenon. An obvious question – how is this truly different from the rat utopia? How is it different from the hermits or the "beautiful ones"?

Remember John Calhoun's conclusion at the end of his experiment: "In the absence of any tension, pressure, or stress they had lost their focus and sense of purpose and identity. With an overabundance of vital resources and no need to do anything to obtain them, the need for societal roles or jobs had faded... These mice, and indeed it could be inferred human beings as well, required conditions of stress, pressure, obstacles, and a clear purpose in order to have a destiny and a desire to engage in society." [16]

ONE FACTOR OF MANY

Some may think I'm being a bit hyperbolic here – a little extreme. And perhaps I am. As I said earlier, the mouse utopia does lend itself to extreme comparisons – so we need to be careful not to take it too far.

However, one thing we can say for sure is that today's urban or "technological" lifestyle seems to be the perfect complement to the sexual revolution that has taken place over the same time frame. They basically thrive off one another. If we think of the new sexual regime as the "software," what this technology has done is to provide the "delivery platform" or hardware to get it to us. And our culture has been soaking in this environment now for decades.

Let me ask this question: What do all these pathologies have in common? What is the smoking gun (so to speak) that connects them all? It is the ultra-low birthrate. Such a thing is completely unnatural – and literally never occurs under "normal" conditions, outside of war, famine or plague. There has to be something very wrong to produce a TFR so low in so many places at once.

It is not just technology. It is not just the sexual revolution. It is not just overcrowding or urbanization. It is some toxic combination of all these things – and it is providing John Glubb's *Age of Decadence* with all the fuel it needs to bury our civilization in a grave of its own digging. And it is happening fast.

The ultra-low birthrate points us in the direction of deep social dysfunction. It should be impossible for such a thing to happen – even in our largest cities. To find so many countries experiencing it, something has to be very wrong. It is almost as if we have invented a lifestyle that is so harmful or poisonous to ourselves that it is literally non-survivable. A dysfunction so deep that our society cannot live through it. And sadly, as we have seen, this syndrome has taken hold throughout the developed world.

A CENTURY OF SELF

In 2002 the BBC produced a fascinating documentary series called *The Century of the Self*. In it they outlined the rise of psychological techniques and manipulation during the twentieth century – tools that were used to sell a new kind of consumerism and self-absorption to the young. Advertising was the new battleground – and every trick and technique were used to market consumables to this growing demographic.[17]

Thus we have a century increasingly obsessed with self. Self-interest, self esteem, self actualization. Advertising and marketing were at the very core of this revolution. "It's all about me" was the byproduct. Not a great way to improve the character of the young.

As Sir John Glubb wrote in *The Fate of Empires,* "Decadence is a moral and spiritual disease, resulting from too long a period of wealth and power, producing cynicism, decline of religion, pessimism and frivolity... Indeed the change might be summarised as being from service to selfishness."[18]

Though it may suit the advertising industry well, this appeal to "self" in commercial after commercial can only serve to accelerate the decline our culture so badly needs to avoid.

CHINA SPEAKS OUT

Getting back to the situation in Asia, there is now confirmation that the phenomenon of 'Grass-eaters' or Herbivore men has gone far beyond just Japan. In 2018 the *South China Morning Post* published a piece entitled: "How herbivores, hermits and stay-at-home men are leaving a generation of Hong Kong women unsatisfied." The article stated that Hong Kong now seems to be following in Japan's footsteps with its very own Herbivore problem.[19]

Dr Paul Wong Wai-ching, an associate professor at the University of Hong Kong, is quoted as saying: "These herbivore men don't connect with others, they don't establish their own families or have children and don't really contribute anything meaningful to society, either tangibly or intangibly. They are like parasites who often live with their parents. So you can imagine how it's going to affect society in the long run, socially and economically." [20]

In 2018 the government of China issued a number of provocative statements about the androgynous male pop idols known in that country as "little fresh meats." As *SBS Australia* says, "They wear make-up, dress in couture and front cosmetic brands. Millions of people are buying whatever they're selling. China's newest male pop stars are young, beautiful, and also known as 'little fresh meat'." [21]

CONTROVERSIAL REMARKS

The thing the Chinese government seemed most concerned about was the state of their nation's masculinity. As another article put it: "China's 'Little Fresh Meat' Idols Spark Masculinity Debate... The cultural phenomenon of celebrating androgynous men is feared by some to be hurting the country's national image... Said to be following a trend of softer masculinity originated by their counterparts in Japan and South Korea and made popular by K-Pop, J-Pop, anime and manga, these idols embody a new form of male beauty, one of a well-groomed, boyish appearance that appeals to female millennials."[22]

China's state-run media *Xinhua* even went so far as to call these pop idols "sissy pants" and "not man, also not woman." They were accused of poisoning the nation's youth. And Japan was blamed for being the original source of the phenomenon.[23]

It is not hugely surprising that the Chinese government would show concern over some of these trends. As I said earlier, many of China's largest cities actually have fertility rates that are among the lowest in the world – below 1.0.[24]

All of these trends have much larger ramifications, of course – ramifications for the entire world. As we shall see in the next chapter, even the idea of the 21st century being the "Asian century" is a concept with a highly dubious foundation. The time has come to take a hard look at China and the "Asian Tiger" economies, to see if their future really is as bright as it has been made out to be.

CHAPTER NINE

CHINA & THE ASIAN TIGERS

Of all the nations in the world, China has one of the most unusual demographic histories that you can find. Of course, many people have heard of the notorious "one child" policy that China implemented from 1980 to 2015 in order to keep a lid on their ever-expanding population. Not only was this policy harsh and draconian at times – with forced abortions and sterilizations, etc. – but it also greatly skewed their demographic profile, with all kinds of dire implications for the future.

Of course there is now a major gender imbalance in the country – with men far outnumbering women – but the Chinese also kept the policy in place for far too long. When they finally relaxed it in 2015, they were expecting a mini "baby boom." What they got instead was a tiny, temporary blip that did little to raise their dangerously low TFR. It was far too little and far too late.

There is simply no coming back from the demographic quagmire that China has created for itself. Of all the nations that we talk about committing "suicide" with their low birthrates, China is probably the poster child for them all.

As the *South China Morning Post* reported in 2019, "Worse than Japan: how China's looming demographic crisis will doom its economic dream... China first began to promote population control in 1973 and introduced its one-child policy in 1980. As a result, its total fertility rate, or births per woman, dropped from 4.54 in 1973 to 2.29 in 1989, then to 1.22 in 2000 and 1.05 (then the lowest in the world) in 2015."[1]

CIVILIZATION ENDING

In 2021 there was an opinion piece in the same newspaper from respected columnist Andy Xie: "Population decline could end China's civilisation as we know it. When will Beijing wake up to the crisis?... The Chinese government recently reported a sharp drop in registered newborns in 2020, 15 per cent down on the year before. This follows three consecutive yearly declines. Instead of a pandemic baby boom, China seems to be having a baby crisis, worse than in far richer countries such as Japan and South Korea."

The piece also noted: "The seeds of the crisis were sown by a development strategy that relied on cheap, plentiful migrant workers... Now, their children don't want to be like them – they would rather surf the internet than have children. The property bubble is only making things worse."[2]

We mentioned in the previous chapter the low birthrates of some of China's largest cities. The latest data suggests Beijing's TFR has now sunk to 0.7 – surely the lowest on the planet.[3] There is no question that bringing millions of migrant workers from the countryside into the cities has played a major role in this collapse. For cramming people into tiny urban apartments is never likely to be too birthrate-friendly.

The peak in China's population is now expected to occur in the mid-2020s and its Working Age cohort is already shrinking by millions of people every year. She is following the pathway of Japan almost to a tee.[4]

The Washington University study published in the *Lancet* now projects that by the year 2100, China's population will literally halve – going from 1.4 billion down to roughly 700 million. Yes – you read that right. Based on the best data we have, China is literally expected to lose 700 million people by the end of this century.[5] It will be the worst human-created bust in recorded history. The size and scope of it is like nothing ever seen before.

THE CRASH OF KOREA

So far, East Asia has not been doing too well in our examination of its birthrates. And that trend is set to continue. The bad news just keeps rolling in.

So tell me – what do you think of when you think about South Korea? Perhaps it is the cars and electronic products manufactured by this ultra-modern nation. Perhaps it is the K-pop idols and bands that have released songs popular around the world. Or perhaps it is the long-simmering tensions with neighboring North Korea which have sometimes threatened to boil over into nuclear conflict.

Sadly, there is one inescapable fact about this Asian "tiger" economy that is set to dominate all others in the decades ahead. And here it is: South Korea has one of the lowest birthrates on the planet. (A shocking 0.92 in 2019. Not even half the replacement rate). And the government recently announced that it expects the population to actually begin shrinking outright by the year 2028.[6]

As one US news outlet commented: "This isn't just a fluke for South Korea -- its demographic crisis has been building for a while. The 2017 rate of 1.05 was also a record low at the time, while the mortality rate jumped to a record high... There is also an increasing trend among men and women to delay or avoid marriage."[7]

THE REVOLUTION STRIKES AGAIN

It appears our old nemesis, the sexual revolution, has its fingerprints all over this situation as well. As the BBC reports: "South Korean women aren't simply choosing to have fewer children – some are opting to forego romantic relationships entirely. An increasing number are choosing never to marry at all, turning their backs on legal partnerships – and even casual relationships – in favour of having independent lives and careers... The shift is part of a rising social phenomenon in South Korea: the Sampo Generation. The word 'sampo' means to give up three things: relationships, marriage and children."

The BBC continues: "Statistics reflect the dramatic shift in culture: marriage rates among South Koreans of childrearing age – both men and women – have plummeted over the last four or five decades. In the 2015 census, fewer than a quarter (23%) of South Korean women aged 25 to 29 said they were married, down steeply from 90% in 1970... And with low birth rates, fewer marriages and longer lives, the trends combine to create a South Korean population that is actually ageing faster than any other developed country." [8]

In 2018, the *Economist* magazine noted this alarming South Korean statistic: "Since the early 1980s more than 3,500 schools have closed; 28 are set to do so this year. The reason is that South Korea is running out of children." [9]

Here is a naked fact that should require no embellishment: You cannot survive a fertility rate that is anywhere close to 1.0. Just think about it for a moment. Every generation that goes by is literally half the size of the one that preceded it. Instead of a family tree, most people end up with a "family stick." Hardly any cousins. Hardly any uncles or aunts. No siblings. A complete cultural, societal, and familial breakdown.

"Demography is destiny" goes the saying – and this is about to play out across East Asia on the grandest scale imaginable.

In 2019, South Korea's *JoongAng Daily* newspaper made the following eye-popping comparison: "In 2017, Korea became the country with the lowest total fertility rate in the world... By comparison, Taiwan's fertility rate is 1.06, Hong Kong's 1.07, Singapore's 1.14." [10]

Now, just think about that for a moment. These are some of the most prominent "Asian tiger" economies in the world. And in 2017 they had fertility rates of 1.06, 1.07 and 1.14 respectively! It is almost as if they are vying with themselves as to who will go into a death-spiral the soonest.

In actual fact, this group of countries have long competed for the title of "lowest fertility on earth." One year it might be Singapore, the next it might be Taiwan, the next it might be

South Korea. So much for the future of the Asian tigers! The economic miracle is coming to an end.

Just a few headlines tell the story:

"Taiwan's Population Will Decline By 2021: Why That's Bad News For It's Tech-Led Economy" *(Forbes)*.

"Hong Kong faces rapid population ageing, shrinking labor force" *(Xinhua)*.

"Singapore is on the brink of a 'demographic time bomb'" *(Business Insider)*.

"How does the shrinking local workforce affect Singapore's economy?" *(Singapore Government)*.

"Asia's worst aging fears begin to come true" *(Nikkei Asian Review)*.

As I have stated before, you cannot build a growing economy on a shrinking population. Your tax base will shrink every year. Your consumer base will shrink every year. Long-term it just cannot be done. A purely export-based economy might get away with it for a time. But even then, the reckoning will one day arrive. This is the very opposite of a long-term success formula. The Asian tigers are running out of rope. And as we have seen, in many ways they are just a bellwether for the entire developed world.

Like the *Titanic,* these nations may sit filling with water for some time before the endgame comes. But come it will. The day of reckoning is near and the piper must be paid.

CHAPTER TEN

CRASH OF CIVILIZATIONS

As stated earlier in this book, we stand today on the edge of the greatest demographic cliff-edge in history – a global synchronized bust of colossal proportions. Nothing like it has ever been seen before – not in Rome, not in Greece, not in Bronze-age Eurasia. This bust dwarfs them all – due to its worldwide scale and the size of the populations involved.

From Germany and Spain in the west to Russia and the Baltics in the east, from China and Japan to the Asian tigers – this will be the crash to rule them all. And it is right on our doorstep. Everyone in our world will be affected. Every investor, every homeowner, every parent, every worker, every boss. Nothing on this earth will escape the effects of this avalanche when it starts rolling down the hill. And in many of these nations the declines have already begun.

Historians say that today's Western civilization is the richest and most prosperous that has ever existed – particularly since it has given the middle classes a lifestyle that former empires could only dream of. But we would do well to remember the saying, "The bigger they are, the harder they fall." We are about to witness this saying come true in real time.

Perhaps you are thinking that the 'BRICS' nations are going to ride in and save the day. But sadly we find that Brazil has a

TFR that is under 1.7 (and has been below replacement for years). And we find too that the entire southern half of India sits well below replacement today. If we are looking to these nations for good news, we are looking in the wrong place (though there is certainly growth in Latin America and South Asia – just not enough to change the overall picture).[1]

But what about the Islamic countries, you say? Don't they have birthrates that are well above average? Well, not enough to make a difference. The birthrates of the richer Muslim countries have actually been falling like a rock in recent years. Today the TFRs of Iran, Turkey, The UAE and Qatar are all below replacement – and others are getting close. There is indeed growth in parts of the Islamic world, but it is nowhere near enough to offset the global declines that are about to hit.[2]

There simply aren't enough words to adequately describe what is coming in the mid-to-late portions of this century. When this wave starts in earnest (within thirty years) it will sweep all before it. Our civilization has survived a lot of things, but it has never seen anything like this. Perhaps a giant asteroid strike or a global nuclear war are the only things that could dwarf it for size. Anything less pales by comparison.

It will start gradually – and get more and more ferocious as it goes. Entire populations will melt away.

Meanwhile, the UN and other large NGOs are now in Africa, spending millions promoting the sexual revolution and birth control – presumably so Africa can be part of the disaster too. There is seemingly no comprehension as to the size of the crash that is coming – nor that we are about to start losing our most precious resource – people. It is human beings that are the earth's most valuable item – and we are about to find ourselves in terrible short supply.

And so the sexual revolution rolls on, claiming new victims while the vultures circle overhead.

A SPERM-COUNT APOCALYPSE

We now turn to something that relates to our main topic, but is a bit of a departure from the themes we have been discussing. In many ways it only serves to raise the alarm another notch higher.

In 1992, a hugely significant study was published in Britain showing a dramatic decline in men's sperm counts and sperm quality throughout the Western world. The paper created an enormous stir, but overall the results were dismissed as flawed or biased in some way. There was apparently no reason to panic just yet.

However, in 2017 a giant meta-analysis was conducted of 185 separate studies involving 43 thousand men from America, Europe, Australia and New Zealand. The results were astounding. As *Scientific American* reported, "The results, published in the journal Human Reproduction Update, showed a 52.4 percent decline in sperm concentration and a 59.3 percent decline in total sperm count." In other words, over a 38-year period, between the years 1973 and 2011, the sperm quality of the average Western male had fallen by over half.[3]

The reaction from the worldwide media was immediate. *Psychology Today* led with the headline, "Going Going Gone? Human Sperm Counts are Plunging," while the BBC declared,

"Sperm Count Drop Could Make Humans Extinct," and the *Financial Times* announced, "'Urgent Wake-Up Call' for Male Health as Sperm Counts Plummet."[4]

But was the issue really that serious? Actually – yes it was.

In 2021 the lead author of the study, Dr. Shanna Swan, published a book on the same topic. It was entitled, *Count Down: How Our Modern World Is Threatening Sperm Counts, Altering Male and Female Reproductive Development, and Imperiling the Future of the Human Race.* The work was full of facts and statistics, receiving great attention from across the globe.[5]

ENDANGERED SPECIES

The publishers issued a number of headline findings, taken from the book itself: "A man today has only half the number of sperm his grandfather had... Worldwide fertility has dropped more than 50% over the past 50 years... In some parts of the world a 20-something woman today is less fertile than her grandmother was at 35... Damage from a man's or pregnant woman's exposure to problematic chemicals and lifestyle influences can harm the reproductive health of multiple future generations... Homo sapiens already fit the U.S. Fish and Wildlife Service's standard to be considered an endangered species."[6]

Every one of these findings would be shocking just in itself – and there is ample proof for every one of them. So what did Dr. Swan believe was largely responsible for this decline? She and her colleagues pointed to a particular class of industrial agents called "endocrine disrupting chemicals" which are mass-produced across the globe.

The most common of these are plastics such as Bisphenol A and phthalates, which are manufactured in enormous quantities every year – and are found throughout the environment we live in, including drink bottles and the linings of canned food. Bisphenol A is actually one of the most commonly produced chemicals on earth, with 3.6 billion tonnes generated each year. Yes – you read that right. 3.6 billion tonnes released into our environment, year in and year out. And Bisphenol A is a proven endocrine disruptor.[7]

INTERSEX FISH

Meanwhile, another possible culprit has also been grabbing headlines. For some years, concerns have been growing that Estrogen may be finding its way into everyday tap water – with similar harmful effects on humans.

In 2016 a report on this was published in the *New Jersey Spotlight:* "Tests on Fish Raise New Concerns About Estrogen Levels in Drinking Water... an investigation of "estrogenic endocrine disruption" among smallmouth and largemouth bass in 19 national wildlife refuges across the Northeast... found intersex in smallmouth bass in all 19 locations at between 60 percent and 100 percent of those fish captured... estrogen contamination in urban areas reflects the construction of wastewater plants that do not treat for the chemicals, and which should not have been permitted in locations that supply public drinking water."

The report continues: "Larry Hajna, a spokesman for the Department of Environmental Protection, said... One of the contributors to the problem is birth-control medication which contains the estrogen that can affect the gender of male fish... He said the DEP is working with other state and local agencies to urge people not to flush birth-control pills down the toilet where the estrogen will find its way into public water systems because treatment plants are not equipped to remove the chemicals." [8]

There it is. Despite the fact that we have a sperm-count drop that is so severe it is threatening our very existence as a species, the authorities can't even keep Estrogen out of the drinking water. (Estrogen so potent that it is actually altering the sex of fish in the wild). What future generations will make of all this is anyone's guess.

In 2018, *The Atlantic* led with this alarming headline: "Sperm Counts Continue to Fall... new research says it's getting worse." The report cited recent studies that show the declines are not even beginning to slow down.[9]

As Dr. Swan states openly in her own book: " If these alarming trends continue unabated, it's difficult to predict what the world will look like in a hundred years. What does this dramatic decline in sperm count portend if it stays on its current trajectory? Does it signal the beginning of the end of the human race – or that we're on the brink of extinction?.. The following is clear: The current state of reproductive affairs can't continue much longer without threatening human survival." [10]

IS IT RESPONSIBLE?

The obvious question to ask here, of course, is whether or not this drastic decline in sperm counts may be the chief reason for the collapse in birthrates over the last sixty years. The question is well worth asking. But looking at the data, it doesn't quite fit. In the West overall, the big collapse in TFRs came very quickly during the 1960s and early 1970s. The majority of this was clearly the result of the sexual revolution and taking the contraceptive pill – because it happened so suddenly.[11]

As Rebecca Eaton, a student in the USA during that period recounts: "It was 1969, and for all the girls and women I knew, life changed profoundly in those four years of college. In 1965 we entered, most of us virginally, as freshmen in knee socks and loafers, looking for husbands and studying art history. We graduated in bell-bottoms [jeans] and white armbands, taking the Pill and attempting to save the world." [12]

As we can see, for Rebecca and many like her, four years was all it took. That's how fast her sexual behavior and worldview were revolutionized. Any drop in sperm quality did not even enter the picture.

And we can clearly see this crash in the birth statistics at the time. For instance, the TFR of Australia fell from 3.41 in 1959 to 2.06 (below replacement) in 1976. That is a pretty sharp drop. But in Canada it was even more extreme. The Canadian TFR fell from 3.94 in 1959 to just 1.98 in 1972 – an incredible collapse in the space of only 13 years. And in France, the TFR fell from 2.91 in 1964 to 1.98 in 1975. Just eleven years from peak to below-replacement.[13]

Obviously, the suddenness of these declines does not really fit with the gradual drop in sperm counts that has occurred over the decades. In fact, most of this crash happened within the space of just fifteen years.[14]

But if sperm counts were not a major factor in the 1960s, what about now? Is it possible that they have been coming into play more and more in recent times? Yes – this is very possible. No doubt it is a big reason why more and more couples today are having to seek special fertility treatments in order to get pregnant. It is not just men's reproductive health that has declined. As Dr. Swan noted, there has been a notable drop-off in the reproductive health of women also. She even says that in some places today, a young 20-something woman is actually less fertile than her grandmother was at 35 years old.[15]

No doubt these factors will play an increasing role over coming decades – making the West's recovery even harder to imagine. In so many ways, it seems, we are literally poisoning our civilization to death.

WHY CIVILIZATIONS FALL

In *The Fate of Empires,* Sir John Glubb relates an interesting anecdote: "Some years ago, a suggestion was submitted to a certain television corporation that a series of talks on Arab history would form an interesting sequence. The proposal was immediately vetoed by the director of programmes with the remark, "What earthly interest could the history of medieval Arabs have for the general public today?"

"Yet, in fact, the history of the Arab imperial age—from conquest through commercialism, to affluence, intellectualism, science and decadence—is an exact precursor of British imperial history and lasted almost exactly the same time. If British historians, a century ago, had devoted serious study to the Arab Empire, they could have foreseen almost everything that has happened in Britain down to 1976." [16]

Of course, today the TFR of Britain stands at 1.65 – and it is staring down the barrel of demographic collapse just like all the rest of the developed world.[17]

In 2011, David P. Goldman released his book, *How Civilizations Die,* which looked at demographic death-spirals down the ages. In it he wrote: "Small civilizations perish for any number of reasons, but great civilizations die only when they no longer want to live." [18] A paraphrase of Toynbee, no doubt.

In his book, Goldman discussed the fall of Sparta, Greece and Rome – and the obvious parallels with today's situation.

In the case of Sparta, the elites apparently kept their birthrates low deliberately, to concentrate wealth in the hands of as few of their offspring as possible. Because of this, by the year 371 BC, Spartan numbers had dwindled to such a degree that their once-fearsome army was actually beaten by a second-rate Theban outfit under the command of Epaminondas. The Greek philosopher Aristotle wrote that the Spartan city-state "sank under a single defeat; the want of men was their ruin." [19]

As far as we know, this was the first time in recorded history that the demise of a great power was blamed on depopulation.

THE FALL OF GREECE & ROME

Meanwhile, the other Greek city-states seemed to be following Sparta's lead. As the Greek general Polybius wrote: "In our time all Greece was visited by a dearth of children and generally a decay of population, owing to which the cities were denuded of inhabitants... This evil grew upon us rapidly, and without attracting attention, by our men becoming perverted to a passion for show and money and the pleasures of an idle life, and accordingly either not marrying at all, or, if they did marry, refusing to rear the children that were born... Little by little the cities become sparsely inhabited and weak."[20]

Clearly, there has been more than one "sexual revolution" in the history of humankind. The Greek geographer Strabo described Greece as "a land entirely deserted; the depopulation begun since long continues. Roman soldiers camp in abandoned houses; Athens is populated by statues."[21]

Demographics seemingly played a part in the eventual fall of Rome also. As John Caldwell, a researcher from the Australian National University, wrote: "Classical literary sources, tombstone inscriptions and skeletal remains have been used by classicists to show that there was probably a decline in the population of the Roman Empire caused by the deliberate control of family numbers... This finding is important as it appears to demonstrate that the fertility transition associated with the modern Industrial Revolution is not unique and may have had predecessors."[22]

The noted Roman scholar A.M. Devine wrote: "There is considerable evidence to show that Roman society in the late

Republic and early Empire was afflicted by a low birthrate... the problem of childlessness was widespread and long-lasting... There is considerable evidence for the existence of marriages which produced no children at all or only one child." [23]

We will probably never know how greatly this ancient "baby bust" actually contributed to Rome's decline. All we can say for sure is that it was something that was present at the time. But the words of Polybius should certainly cause echoes of alarm in our own ears. His ancient observation that "becoming perverted to a passion for show and money and the pleasures of an idle life" was something that undermined the desire for a family and children – is surely a warning to us today. [24] Perhaps history does sometimes repeat, after all.

WHAT MAY BE LOST?

Some years ago I stood under the remains of a huge Roman aqueduct in the south of France. This giant structure had stood, frozen in time, for something like 2000 years. It was an engineering marvel – made with a skill so precise that today we would need laser-levels and high-tech wizardry to even have a chance of emulating its function.

When Rome fell, the world lost all the skills that made this marvel possible. For centuries, people lived and died, ate and slept, in the shadow of a technology that they could no longer wield – or even comprehend. They could gape in wonder at the beauty of it, but the brilliance and precision that created it was utterly lost. Progress literally went backwards for hundreds of years – in fact, an entire millennium.

I wonder if the same thing will happen when our own civilization comes tumbling down (for tumble it will). I wonder what kind of world our great-great-great grandchildren will inherit. Will it be a culture that is slowly losing everything that has been built for thousands of years? Will our grandchildren's grandchildren stand beneath our giant structures, mouth agape, wondering how and why they were ever constructed – much as we ponder the Aztec ruins or the pyramids of Giza? Will historians one day study the "Great Collapse of the 21st Century" just as we study the fall of Rome today?

Most great empires go out, not with a bang, but a whimper. They rot themselves out internally for years before they finally fall.

I have come to believe that civilizations die because in some way, somehow, they deserve to die. There is something intrinsically cancerous at the heart of them, something hollowing them out, something they cannot survive. There is a sense that they are slowly poisoning themselves to death – not physically – but somehow spiritually. These are no longer the people who built the palace they live in. In some vital way they have come to resemble the spoiled rich kids who inherit dad's money but can't help losing it all.

We are staring down the barrel of a civilizational crash so enormous that it will make the fall of Rome seem like a popgun by comparison – because the scale of it is so incredibly vast. And time is running out.

CHAPTER ELEVEN

AMERICA'S LAST HOPE

If you were to ask me whether there is any chance that Western Europe will survive the coming storm, my answer, sadly, would be, "No." There is nothing about Europe that gives me any sense that it can reform itself in time to prevent calamity – especially since the declines have already begun.

If you ask me the same question concerning Eastern Europe, would my answer be any different? Unfortunately not. Again, there is nothing about the former Soviet states that gives me any hope that they can stop the rot in time.

And the same is true of East Asia – with its economic titans – China, Japan and South Korea. Do they have time to alter course? Again the answer is, "No." The crisis is already upon them. Nothing can be done. It would be like asking the *Titanic* to change course after it has already hit the iceberg.

However, there is one major nation that I have deliberately saved until last in this discussion. And it is not because they are in particularly great demographic shape. (Though they are not at a critical stage just yet). But that is not the reason I have left them to last.

Of course, the nation I am referring to is the United States. And the reason I think they are a bit of a special case is not because of demography, but rather because of religion. Of all the nations in the West today, the USA is seemingly the only one that has not completely lost its grasp on religious faith. (Though there are worrying signs of decay). And this one factor does have the potential to make a difference in the fate of the country.

A TROUBLED LAND

Despite being the leading superpower of this era, America is showing many of the signs of late-stage decline that we have discussed in this book. For the middle classes, wages have stagnated (in real terms) since the 1970s. Income inequality is rampant and growing. Drug deaths are at record highs. Birthrates are at record lows (hovering around 1.65).[1] On top of all this, the sexual revolution has taken a heavy toll on the fabric of society and family life. America is not the nation it used to be.

Moreover, political divisions in the country have now become so extreme that in early 2022, two serious non-fiction books were published predicting a new civil war in the United States (one authored by a political scientist from UC San Diego).[2] People talk openly of a "national divorce."

As we have seen, such intractable schisms and divisions are just further signs of late-stage decay. To repeat the words of Sir John Glubb: "The Byzantines spent the last fifty years of their history in fighting one another in repeated civil wars... True to the normal course followed by nations in decline, internal differences are not reconciled in an attempt to save the nation.

On the contrary, internal rivalries become more acute, as the nation becomes weaker."[3]

Today we also see the terrible pessimism that Glubb spoke of, infecting not just America, but much of the Western world. People are worried about the future, and their outlook for their own nation is becoming bleaker. Dark times are ahead, and many can feel it in their bones.

WHY FAITH MATTERS

For many years, demographers have noted the striking correlation between high religious devotion and high birthrates. In 2010, Eric Kaufmann, a professor from the University of London, released a book entitled, *Shall the Religious Inherit the Earth?: Demography and Politics in the Twenty-First Century*. As you may guess from the title, the book's main point was that, as populations spiral into decline across the developed world, it will be the religious who slowly take over – due to their higher birthrates.

Kaufmann writes: "Even if everyone else died off, homo religiosus would endure... People are increasingly failing to replace themselves and the openly non-religious among them are displaying the lowest fertility rates ever recorded in human history... Those embracing the here and now are spearheading population decline, but individuals who shun this world are relatively immune to it."[4]

Kaufmann gives examples of two groups with some of the highest birthrates on earth – both of them very religious: "The Old Order Amish, for instance, double in population every twenty years. They numbered just 5,000 in 1900, but have close to a quarter million members today. In the period 1997–2003 alone, sixty-six new Amish colonies formed. Only the fastest-growing non-denominational megachurches can match their growth rate.

"Consider the ultra-orthodox Jews, a larger group who – at least in Israel – occupy a much smaller pond... In Britain, they constitute only 17 percent of Jews but account for 75 percent of Jewish births. In Israel, they have increased from a few percent of Jewish schoolchildren in 1950 to a third of all Jewish pupils. In both places, the Haredi may be the majority by 2050 and certainly by 2100."[5]

Even in America, it is very noticeable that the more religious states have a higher TFR than the least religious.[6] After all, the Bible does say, "Be fruitful and multiply" (Genesis 1:22). What this means is that, over time, the least religious populations tend to lose out to the more religious.

UNIQUE MAKEUP

As mentioned earlier, America is different from all the other Western nations when it comes to religious faith. Christianity still plays an important role in the life of the average American – far more so than any other Western power.[7] However, even the USA has seen a decline in faith over recent decades.

In 2019, Pew Research published the following report: "In U.S., Decline of Christianity Continues at Rapid Pace... in 2018 and 2019, 65% of American adults describe themselves as Christians when asked about their religion, down 12 percentage points over the past decade. Meanwhile, the religiously unaffiliated share of the population, consisting of people who describe their religious identity as atheist, agnostic or "nothing in particular," now stands at 26%, up from 17% in 2009."[8]

As the authors of *Empty Planet* wrote: "We don't need to get into the various reasons that have been put forward for why faith is weakening in many societies, though it's worth pointing out that the same forces that reduce fertility—rising affluence, improved education, the emancipation of women, the weakening influence of kin—also weaken the power of organized religion."[9]

Isn't that interesting? Their evidence shows that the very trends we have been discussing not only send birthrates lower, but they also affect religious faith the same way. Both suffer together. This has been seen in nation after nation – including America.

The *Empty Planet* authors continue: "Three WIN/Gallup polls, taken in 2008, 2009, and 2015, asked respondents whether they felt religious or not. In Malawi and Niger—which, as we've seen, have among the highest fertility rates in the world —99 percent of those polled answered yes. Only 39 percent said yes in Spain, which is now considered one of the least religious countries in the world."[10]

Meanwhile, Professor Kaufmann's summary of population trends over the next 100 years is one of the most succinct that I have come across: "The world is in the midst of an unprecedented shift from population growth to decline. Europe is leading the way, but East Asia is aging more quickly and may overtake it, while other parts of the world – especially India, Southeast Asia and Latin America – are treading the same path. These changes are driven by rising prosperity, women's education, urbanisation and birth control." [11]

THE PEAK IS NIGH

Let's leave the subject of religion for a moment to focus on U.S. demography. Speaking in purely demographic terms, America is in a similar situation to nations like France, Australia, Norway and Sweden. The Washington University study tells us that the United States is "projected to have population growth until mid-century, followed by a moderate decline of less than 10% of the peak population by 2100." [12]

In other words, like other "best of the West" nations, America's population is expected to peak around 2050 and then decline steadily after that (taking immigration and everything else into account). Unlike Japan and China, which will fall precipitously, America's decline is set to be only moderate at first.

This all sounds rather benign, but let me remind you: 2050 is only a little over 25 years away. And we are talking about the greatest military power the world has ever known – the leading democracy of our civilization. Around 2050, this dominant power will begin to decline in numbers – and it is never coming back. There is no fairy-tale ending to this story. Like all the other nations, once this decline sets in it can likely never be stopped. And not only that, but severe economic problems are certain to arise well before the peak.

This is why the evidence points to a colossal financial meltdown within thirty years. It is likely to be Japan times a hundred. You can paper over these cracks for awhile, but sooner or later the piper must be paid. This will be a global synchronized bust on a scale never seen before. And once it starts it is never going away.

A GLIMMER OF HOPE?

So why have I marked out the United States as different – if her fate is largely the same as others? Why have I bothered to highlight her greater levels of religious faith – when it is unlikely to make much difference in the long run?

Well, there is a little word called "hope," and even though it may be just a tiny speck, it is still worth discussing. The fact is, there is actually good historic precedent for thinking that America may make a sudden dramatic U-turn in her spiritual path – for she has done so many times before.

What I am speaking about here, of course, is America's long history of "Great Awakenings" – a history only partially shared by other countries. Each time one of these religious revivals swept over the land, it refreshed not just people's faith, but also the very soul of the nation itself.

AWAKENINGS OF OLD

It is remarkable to look at the great waves of Christian revival that have swept over America since its founding – waves that have shaped the country and helped make her the superpower she is today. A careful historian can discern five great religious revivals in U.S. history – perhaps even six. In 1741 came what is known as the First Great Awakening – which set the stage for all that would follow.

In 1801 came the Second Great Awakening, in 1857 the Third, and so on – right up to recent times. Basically, these waves seemed to come at roughly 50-year intervals – every second generation or so. In the middle of the twentieth century, following World War II, came the fifth great wave, led by preachers such as Billy Graham and Oral Roberts. This was the era of the "tent evangelists" who crisscrossed the country preaching up a storm in town after town.

Sadly, this entire wave was largely missed by most of the other Western nations (though they had kept up with some of the others). America now stood alone – the only "revival country" left in the West. And this explains so much about what makes America different. The embers that have died out in other places still glow beneath the surface in America, awaiting a new breeze that will set them aflame once again. But the obstacles and hindrances are now greater than ever.

When I lived in the United States during the early 2000s, I used to warn my American audiences of what would happen if the USA missed its next "window" of revival – what disasters would follow if this chain was broken. America has been kept alive by faith – not by constitutions. People simply do not realize the great debt that the USA – and all the other Western nations – owe to Christianity, and the way it has shaped our culture.

It is no coincidence that as Christianity has been dying in the West, so our civilization has been dying too.

ONE LAST WAVE?

Interestingly, there was a kind of "mini-Awakening" in America during the early 1970s as a response to the hippy culture of that time. It was known as the Jesus Movement – part of what was called the "Charismatic renewal" of the era.[13] Basically it was a kind-of street revival, a long-haired version of Christianity that brought thousands and thousands of young people into the fold – mainly in America and a few other Western countries. The last gasp of a dying polity perhaps – or the precursor of something new?

There have been a number of commentators that have stated our need for a new religious revival in the West today. Among them was the historian Arnold J. Toynbee, who famously declared that only a "revival in religion" can save Western civilization from its current terminal path.[14]

In this he was echoed by Sir John Glubb, author of *The Fate of Empires,* who wrote: "At the height of vice and frivolity the seeds of religious revival are quietly sown. After, perhaps, several generations (or even centuries) of suffering, the impoverished nation has been purged of its selfishness and its love of money, religion regains its sway and a new era sets in. 'It is good for me that I have been afflicted,' said the psalmist, 'that I might learn Thy Statutes.'"[15]

So is there any chance that America might experience such a "purging" in the near future? Is there hope for one last Great Awakening before the end?

From my own studies of these cycles in the U.S., it seems there may be one last tiny glimmer of hope for an Awakening around the late 2020s or early 2030s. But for that to occur, as Sir John Glubb himself intimated, it appears the nation may need to go through some terrible ordeal or "purging" first. Either way, it seems to me, the West is in for a nasty shakeup over the next few decades. In fact, there is no nation in the entire developed or semi-developed world that will escape the storm that is coming.

THE ENDGAME LOOMS

In closing this book, there is one thing that I want to emphasize. The picture we are painting of the future here is not guesswork. We are not working off some arcane model whose predictions change with the wind. We are in the "births, deaths and migrations" business here. The numbers are unequivocal and the declines have already begun.

No doubt there will be some variation – a few data points out here and there. Ten million up, ten million down. But the overall picture remains the same. The countries that are in trouble will always be the countries that are in trouble. Nothing can change that now.

There is no question that our civilization is facing the greatest bust in the history of the planet. The size and scope of it staggers the imagination. And the fact that so many great powers will enter the vortex around the same time only makes the situation worse. It will be a coordinated catastrophe. Every developed region of the earth will succumb within the same couple of decades.

A CRASH LIKE NO OTHER

I am convinced that the first downdraft of this disaster will be financial and economic in nature. No doubt we are already feeling these effects now. As I have said, the peak in the economy is likely to come years before the actual peak in population.

Immense efforts will be made by the Central Banks of the world to stave off these disasters. Billions will be printed – then trillions – right across the globe. In fact, isn't that what we are already seeing? Isn't the financial world in so many ways already following the pathway of Japan?

But these efforts will ultimately founder. Some region somewhere will fail in this giant prop-up job – perhaps China, perhaps Japan, or Europe, or America. The first domino will tumble. And then comes the waterfall.

I have spoken about this meltdown coming within thirty years. But it wouldn't surprise me at all if it starts within five years or less. The aging regions of the earth look to be in serious trouble already, to my eyes.

Of course, the problem with this particular depression is that it will never truly end. There will be bailouts galore and brief lulls for a year or two. But overall, once it begins, I expect this "greatest recession" to go on virtually forever. Why should it stop, when the population is continuing to decline?

Meanwhile, from this decade of the 2020s onward, nation after nation will be reaching its population peak and then sliding down the other side. Some will slide quickly, others at a measured pace. But slide they will. And so the momentum will accelerate to the downside. A never-ending race to the bottom.

At this point we will very likely see economic migrations on a mass scale. The least-bad economies will tend to gain the vast majority of the young and educated, while the basket-case countries will simply empty out. Entire regions may be left with only the elderly and frail. The young professionals will crowd into smaller and smaller enclaves as the decline goes on. "Last man standing" gets a plastic medallion.

CLOSING REMARKS

The sun is setting on what is probably the greatest civilization the world has ever known. Like many that have gone before, she is to die by her own hand – but slowly. She has lost her grip on faith, and thus stands ready to lose all else besides. This is as much a spiritual crisis as anything. A civilization founded on Christianity cannot survive the loss of that vital faith. And survive it she will not. The rot at her heart has become too great.

Many will run to and fro, searching for this solution or that. Every possible remedy will be tried. But all this is just putting out deckchairs on the *Titanic*. Nothing can make up for a declining population. Nothing.

It may be that the invention of the birth-control pill itself is found to be non-survivable. Can our species live through something that rewires our entire sexual, social and reproductive world in such a profound way? The answer may well be, "No – it cannot." Or maybe the "pill" was just a symptom of a much deeper disease.

Would our fate be any different today if it had never been released at all? Or would Glubb's *Age of Decadence* have taken our civilization out regardless of anything science had to offer? Clearly, our culture has all kinds of toxic pathologies quite apart from this one. And if I'm honest, I would have to say that any two of these deep dysfunctions could take us out without even raising a sweat. The *Fate of Empires* wins again.

As our discussion draws to a close, let us look with honest eyes at the squalid state of our once-world-beating culture today.

Riven by spiritual malaise, up to its eyeballs in debt, mesmerized by philosophies and beliefs so foolish and unnatural that they will become the laughing-stock of ages, our civilization sinks down to its grave. A riddle, wrapped in a mystery, inside an enigma – as the old saying goes – she will go out, not with a bang, but a whimper.

And so, when your great-great-grandchildren ask you what was the cause of the great collapse, you can tell them:

We lost our faith.

We lost our children.

We lost our civilization.

In that order.

REFERENCES & QUOTATIONS

Chapter One

1. Prof Stein Emil Vollset, DrPH et al., *The Lancet,* 2020, thelancet.com/article/S0140-6736(20)30677-2/fulltext

2. *Ibid.*

3. Millennium Edition, *'Myths of the 20th century,'* New York Times, January 1, 2000.

4. Prof Stein Emil Vollset, DrPH et al., *The Lancet,* 2020, thelancet.com/article/S0140-6736(20)30677-2/fulltext

5. *'World Population Could Peak Decades Ahead of U.N. Forecast, Study Asserts,'* New York Times, 2020. nytimes.com/2020/07/14/world/americas/global-population-trends.html

Chapter Two

1. Arnold Joseph Toynbee, *'Civilization on Trial,'* 1948.

2. Sir John Bagot Glubb, KCB, *'The Fate of Empires and Search for Survival,'* 1978, Introduction.

3. *Ibid.,* pg 2-4.

4. *Ibid.,* pg 9.

5. Sir John Bagot Glubb, KCB, *'The Fate of Empires and Search for Survival,'* 1978, pg 10.

6. *Ibid.,* pg 11-12.

7. *Ibid.,* pg 12-14.

8. *Ibid.,* pg 11.

Chapter Three

1. Sir John Bagot Glubb, KCB, *'The Fate of Empires and Search for Survival,'* 1978, pg 14.

2. *Ibid.,* pg 15-16.

3. *Historical Statistics of the United States – Colonial Times to 1970 – Part 1* (Bicentennial ed.), U.S. Department of Commerce. Bureau of Census, 1975, pp. 19, 50

4. NPR, *'The Great Bluff That Led To A 'Magical' Pill And A Sexual Revolution,'* 2014, www.npr.org/sections/health-shots/2014/10/07/354103536/

5. Jonathan Eig, *'The Birth of the Pill: How Four Pioneers Reinvented Sex and Launched a Revolution,'* 2014.

6. Betsey Stevenson and Justin Wolfers, *'The Paradox of Declining Female Happiness,'* IZA 2009, ftp.iza.org/dp4200.pdf

7. Maureen Cleave, *'How does a Beatle live?'* London Evening Standard, 4 March 1966.

8. Sir John Bagot Glubb, KCB, *'The Fate of Empires and Search for Survival,'* 1978, pg 14.

9. Chris Bodenner, *'The Breakdown of the Black Family,' Cont'd,* The Atlantic, Oct 12, 2015, theatlantic.com/national/archive/2015/10/the-breakdown-of-the-black-family-contd/626229/

10. Sir John Bagot Glubb, KCB, *'The Fate of Empires and Search for Survival,'* 1978, pg 15.

11. *'UPenn Swimmer's Parent Says Female Swimmers are 'Really Unhappy' with Transgender Teammate Situation,'* National Review, January 21, 2022.

12. *'Imagine (John Lennon song),'* wikipedia.org/wiki/Imagine_(John_Lennon_song)

13. Sir John Bagot Glubb, KCB, *'The Fate of Empires and Search for Survival,'* 1978, pg 15, 17.

14. *Ibid.,* pg 20, 22, 24.

Chapter Four

1. Betsey Stevenson and Justin Wolfers, *'The Paradox of Declining Female Happiness,'* IZA 2009, ftp.iza.org/dp4200.pdf

2. Margarita Delgado Perez and Massimo Livi-Bacci, *'Fertility in Italy and Spain: The Lowest in the World,'* Family Planning Perspectives Vol. 24, No. 4, 1992, Guttmacher Institute, doi.org/10.2307/2136019

3. *'Fertility rate: 'Jaw-dropping' global crash in children being born,'* BBC, 15 July 2020, bbc.com/news/health-53409521

4. Prof Stein Emil Vollset, DrPH et al., *The Lancet,* 2020, thelancet.com/article/S0140-6736(20)30677-2/fulltext

5. *Ibid.*

6. *'Pregnancy after 35: What are the risks?'* Medical News Today, Jun 2017, medicalnewstoday.com/articles/317861

7. *'Having a Baby After Age 35: How Aging Affects Fertility and Pregnancy,'* American College of Obstetricians and Gynecologists,

acog.org/womens-health/faqs/having-a-baby-after-age-35-how-aging-affects-fertility-and-pregnancy

8. *'Pregnancy after 35: What are the risks?'* Medical News Today, Jun 2017, medicalnewstoday.com/articles/317861

9. *What's the Average Person's Number of Sexual Partners?'* Healthline, 2019, healthline.com/health/healthy-sex/average-number-of-sexual-partners

10. Aubrey Hirsch, *'Women are increasingly unhappy,'* Vox, Nov 20, 2019, vox.com/the-highlight/2019/11/13/20959863/

11. Betsey Stevenson and Justin Wolfers, *'The Paradox of Declining Female Happiness,'* IZA 2009, ftp.iza.org/dp4200.pdf

12. *'The Economic Impact of Falling Birth Rates,'* International Strategic Analysis, 12 September 2019, isa-world.com/news/

13. *Ibid.*

14. *Fertility statistics - European Commission*, Eurostat, ec.europa.eu/eurostat/statistics-explained/index.php?title=Fertility_statistics

15. *Development of births,* Federal Statistical Office of Germany, destatis.de/EN/Themes/Society-Environment/Population/Births/_node.html

16. *Ibid.*

17. *Ibid.*

18. *'Not so fast,'* The Economist, May 28th, 2016, economist.com/special-report/2016/05/26/not-so-fast

19. *'Working-age population expected to decrease by 4 to 6 million by 2035,'* Federal Statistical Office of Germany, 27 June 2019, destatis.de/EN/Press/2019/06/PE19_242_12411.html

20. *Fertility statistics - European Commission*, Eurostat, ec.europa.eu/eurostat/statistics-explained/index.php?title=Fertility_statistics

21. *'Not so fast,'* The Economist, May 28th, 2016, economist.com/special-report/2016/05/26/not-so-fast

22. Darrell Bricker and John Ibbitson, *'Empty Planet: The Shock of Global Population Decline,'* 2019, Location: 1,061.

23. *'Fecund Foreigners?'* The Economist, 30 April 2016. economist.com/news/international/21697819-immigrants-do-less-raise-birth-rates-generally-believed-fecund-foreigners

24. *'Global elderly care in crisis,'* The Lancet, March 15, 2014, doi.org/10.1016/S0140-6736(14)60463-3

25. *Ibid.*

Chapter Five

1. Darrell Bricker and John Ibbitson, *'Empty Planet: The Shock of Global Population Decline,'* 2019, Location: 80.

2. *Ibid.,* Location: 140.

3. *Ibid.,* Location: 1,542.

4. *'The Economic Impact of Falling Birth Rates,'* International Strategic Analysis, 12 September 2019, isa-world.com/news/

5. *'Toys R Us' baby problem is everybody's baby problem,'* Washington Post, March 15th, 2018, washingtonpost.com/news/wonk/wp/2018/03/15/toys-r-uss-baby-problem-is-everybodys-baby-problem/

6. *Ibid.*

Chapter Six

1. *State Statistics Service of Ukraine,* ukrstat.gov.ua/

2. *Ibid.*

3. *'Bulgaria, Latvia, Poland, and Ukraine projected to experience largest declines in workforce,'* Emerging Europe, July 15, 2019, emerging-europe.com/news/bulgaria-latvia-poland-and-ukraine-projected-to-experience-largest-declines-in-workforce/

4. *'Top Russian Official Warns of 'Catastrophic' Population Loss,'* Moscow Times, July 3 2019, themoscowtimes.com/2019/07/03/top-russian-official-warns-of-catastrophic-population-loss-a66259

5. *'UN Predicts Russia's Population Could Halve By 2100,'* Moscow Times, June 18 2019, themoscowtimes.com/2019/06/18/un-predicts-russias-population-could-halve-2100-a66035

6. *Federal State Statistics Service,* Rosstat, rosstat.gov.ru

7. *Ibid.*

8. *'Rising Mortality Rates Challenge Russia's Efforts To Kick-Start Population Growth,'* Radio Free Europe, April 04 2019, rferl.org/a/29861882.html

9. *'Russia's demographic problem,'* Financial Observer, 22.05.2019, financialobserver.eu/cse-and-cis/russias-demographic-problem/

10. Darrell Bricker and John Ibbitson, *'Empty Planet: The Shock of Global Population Decline,'* 2019, Location: 80.

11. *'Russia and weapons of mass destruction,'* wikipedia.org/wiki/Russia_and_weapons_of_mass_destruction

12. *'The emptying East of Europe,'* Mercatornet, 2019, mercatornet.com/mobile/view/the-empty-east-of-europe

13. *'Bye-Bye Balkans: A Region in Critical Demographic Decline,'* Balkan Insight, 2019, balkaninsight.com/2019/10/14/bye-bye-balkans-a-region-in-critical-demographic-decline/

Chapter Seven

1. *'Japans population projected to plunge to 88 million by 2065,'* Japan Times, 2017, japantimes.co.jp/news/2017/04/10/national/social-issues/japans-population-projected-plunge-88-million-2065/

2. *Ibid.*

3. Jim Rickards, *'Japan's in the middle of its 3rd 'lost decade' and a recovery is nowhere in sight,'* The Daily Reckoning Mar 24, 2016, businessinsider.com/japans-3rd-lost-decade-recovery-nowhere-in-sight-2016-3

4. *Ibid.*

5. *'United Nations Statistics Division – Demographic and Social Statistics,'* Unstats.un.org.

6. *'How Japan's ageing population is shrinking GDP,'* Financial Times, 2018, ft.com/content/7ce47bd0-545f-11e8-b3ee-41e0209208ec

7. *Ibid.*

8. *'Craving Freedom, Japan's Women Opt Out of Marriage,'* New York Times, August 3 2019, nytimes.com/2019/08/03/world/asia/japan-single-women-marriage.html

9. *Ibid.*

10. *Ibid.*

11. *'No Sex Please – We're Japanese,'* BBC, 2013, bbc.com

12. Kevin Wu, *'Rise of the herbivore men,'* The Stony Brook Press, Apr 22 2019, sbpress.com/2019/04/herbivore-men

13. *'Japan's Generation XX,'* The Independent, 13 June 2009, independent.co.uk/news/world/asia/japans-generation-xx-1704155.html

14. *'In Japan, 'Herbivore' Boys Subvert Ideas Of Manhood,'* NPR, November 25, 2009, text.npr.org/s.php?sId=120696816

15. Kevin Wu, *'Rise of the herbivore men,'* The Stony Brook Press, Apr 22 2019, sbpress.com/2019/04/herbivore-men

16. *'The Japanese government is trying to find your perfect match,'* CNN, September 27, 2016, money.cnn.com/2016/09/21/news/economy/japan-government-dating-services/index.html

17. *'List of countries by suicide rate,'* wikipedia.org/wiki/List_of_countries_by_suicide_rate

18. *'Number of abandoned homes in Japan edges up to record high of nearly 8.5 million,'* The Japan Times, 26 Apr 2019, japantimes.co.jp/news/2019/04/26/national/number-abandoned-homes-japan-edges-record-high-nearly-8-5-million/

19. CNN and The Pulitzer Center on Crisis Reporting, *'Japan has so many vacant homes it's giving them away,'* CNN, January 15, 2019, edition.cnn.com/2018/12/05/asia/japan-vacant-akiya-ghost-homes/index.html

20. *'Japans population projected to plunge to 88 million by 2065,'* Japan Times, 2017, japantimes.co.jp/news/2017/04/10/national/social-issues/japans-population-projected-plunge-88-million-2065/

Chapter Eight

1. Edmund Ramsden & Jon Adams, *'Escaping the Laboratory: The Rodent Experiments of John B. Calhoun & Their Cultural Influence.'* LSE, 2008. Pg 1.

2. *Ibid.,* pg 1.

3. *Ibid.,* pg 1.

4. *'John B. Calhoun,'* retrieved 25 May 2014. wikipedia.org/wiki/John_B._Calhoun

5. John B Calhoun MD, *'Death Squared: The Explosive Growth and Demise of a Mouse Population,'* 1973.

6. *Ibid.*

7. *Ibid.*

8. Brent Swancer, *'The Amazing Rise and Fall of a Rodent Utopia,'* Mysterious Universe, March 4, 2015, mysteriousuniverse.org/2015/03/the-amazing-rise-and-fall-of-a-rodent-utopia/

9. *Ibid.*

10. *Ibid.*

11. Brent Swancer, *'The Amazing Rise and Fall of a Rodent Utopia,'* Mysterious Universe, March 4, 2015, mysteriousuniverse.org/2015/03/the-amazing-rise-and-fall-of-a-rodent-utopia/

12. *Ibid.*

13. *Ibid.*

14. Edmund Ramsden & Jon Adams, *'Escaping the Laboratory: The Rodent Experiments of John B. Calhoun & Their Cultural Influence.'* LSE, 2008, pg 1.

15. Nicholas Eberstadt, *'Men Without Work,'* 2016, Introduction.

16. Brent Swancer, *'The Amazing Rise and Fall of a Rodent Utopia,'* Mysterious Universe, March 4, 2015, mysteriousuniverse.org/2015/03/the-amazing-rise-and-fall-of-a-rodent-utopia/

17. *'The Century of the Self,'* BBC, 2002, bbc.com

18. Sir John Bagot Glubb, KCB, *'The Fate of Empires and Search for Survival,'* 1978, pg 9.

19. *'How herbivores, hermits and stay-at-home men are leaving a generation of Hong Kong women unsatisfied,'* South China Morning Post, 2018, amp.scmp.com/lifestyle/families/article/2147743/how-herbivores-hermits-and-stay-home-men-are-leaving-generation

20. *Ibid.*

21. *'Who are 'little fresh meat' idols and why are they worth big money?'* SBS Australia, 12 Jul 2018, sbs.com.au/popasia/blog/2018/07/12/who-are-little-fresh-meat-idols-and-why-are-they-worth-big-money

22. *'China's 'Little Fresh Meat' Idols Spark Masculinity Debate,'* Culture Trip, 25 September 2018, theculturetrip.com/asia/china/articles/chinas-little-fresh-meat-idols-spark-masculinity-debate/

23. *'Xinhua Mocks 'Sissy Pants' Male Idols,'* Sixth Tone, Sep 08, 2018, sixthtone.com/news/1002883/

24. *'China's birthrate just hit another record low. But the worst is yet to come,'* CNN, December 2, 2021, edition.cnn.com/2021/12/01/china/china-birthrate-2020-mic-intl-hnk/index.html

Chapter Nine

1. *'Worse than Japan: how China's looming demographic crisis will doom its economic dream,'* South China Morning Post, 2019, scmp.com/comment/insight-opinion/asia/article/2180421/worse-japan-how-chinas-looming-demographic-crisis-will

2. Andy Xie, *'Population decline could end China's civilisation as we know it. When will Beijing wake up to the crisis?'* South China Morning Post, 3 Mar, 2021,

scmp.com/comment/opinion/article/3123726/population-decline-could-end-chinas-civilisation-we-know-it-when

3. *'China's birthrate just hit another record low. But the worst is yet to come,'* CNN, December 2, 2021, edition.cnn.com/2021/12/01/china/china-birthrate-2020-mic-intl-hnk/index.html

4. *Worse than Japan: how China's looming demographic crisis will doom its economic dream,'* South China Morning Post, 2019, scmp.com/comment/insight-opinion/asia/article/2180421/worse-japan-how-chinas-looming-demographic-crisis-will

5. Prof Stein Emil Vollset, DrPH et al., *The Lancet,* 2020, thelancet.com/article/S0140-6736(20)30677-2/fulltext

6. *'South Korea's population will start shrinking in less than a decade,'* Quartz, March 29, 2019, qz.com/1583313/south-korea-population-to-peak-in-2028

7. *'South Korea's fertility rate falls to record low,'* CNN, August 29, 2019, edition.cnn.com/2019/08/29/asia/south-korea-fertility-intl-hnk-trnd/index.html

8. *'South Korea's population paradox,'* BBC, 15th October 2019, bbc.com/worklife/article/20191010-south-koreas-population-paradox

9. *'South Korea's fertility rate is the lowest in the world,'* The Economist, 30 June 2018, economist.com/asia/2018/06/30/south-koreas-fertility-rate-is-the-lowest-in-the-world

10. *'Total fertility rate in Korea falls below 1, lower than any other nation,' JoongAng Daily,* August 28, 2019, koreajoongangdaily.joins.com/news/article/article.aspx?aid=3067335

Chapter Ten

1. Prof Stein Emil Vollset, DrPH et al., *The Lancet,* 2020, thelancet.com/article/S0140-6736(20)30677-2/fulltext

2. *Ibid.*

3. Hagai Levine et al., *'Temporal trends in sperm count: a systematic review and meta-regression analysis,'* Human Reproduction Update, Volume 23, Issue 6, November-December 2017, Pages 646–659, doi.org/10.1093/humupd/dmx022

4. Shanna H. Swan and Stacey Colino, *'Count Down,'* 2021, Prologue.

5. *Ibid.*

6. *Ibid.,* Cover.

7. *'Are we poisoning our children with plastic?'* The Guardian, 19 Feb 2018, theguardian.com/lifeandstyle/2018/feb/19/are-we-poisoning-our-children-with-plastic

8. *'Tests on Fish Raise New Concerns About Estrogen Levels in Drinking Water,'* New Jersey Spotlight, Feb 9 2016, njspotlight.com/2016/02/16-02-08-tests-on-fish-raise-new-concerns-on-estrogen-contamination-of-drinking-water/

9. *'Sperm Counts Continue to Fall,'* The Atlantic, Oct 2018, theatlantic.com/family/archive/2018/10/sperm-counts-continue-to-fall/572794/

10. Shanna H. Swan and Stacey Colino, *'Count Down,'* 2021, Prologue.

11. *Fertility Rate, Total for the United States,* St. Louis Fed, fred.stlouisfed.org/series/SPDYNTFRTINUSA

12. Rebecca Eaton, *'Making Masterpiece: 25 Years Behind the Scenes at Masterpiece Theatre and Mystery!'* PBS.

13. *Fertility rate, total (births per woman),* The World Bank, data.worldbank.org/indicator/SP.DYN.TFRT.IN

14. *Ibid.*

15. Shanna H. Swan and Stacey Colino, *'Count Down,'* 2021, Cover.

16. Sir John Bagot Glubb, KCB, *'The Fate of Empires and Search for Survival,'* 1978, pg 21.

17. Prof Stein Emil Vollset, DrPH et al., *The Lancet,* 2020, thelancet.com/article/S0140-6736(20)30677-2/fulltext

18. David P. Goldman, *'How Civilizations Die,'* 2011, pg 122.

19. *Ibid.,* pg 120.

20. Polybius, *'The Histories Vol.II,'* trans. Evelyn S. Shuckburg (London MacMillan, 1889), 511.

21. David P. Goldman, *'How Civilizations Die,'* 2011, pg 130.

22. Caldwell, J.C., Journal of Population Research (2004) 21: 1, doi.org/10.1007/BF03032208

23. A. M. Devine, *'The Low Birth-Rate in Ancient Rome: A Possible Contributing Factor.'* Rheinisches Museum für Philologie, Neue Folge, 128. Bd., H. 3/4 (1985), pg. 313.

24. Polybius, *'The Histories Vol.II,'* trans. Evelyn S. Shuckburg (London MacMillan, 1889), 511.

Chapter Eleven

1. *Fertility rate, total (births per woman) - United States,* The World Bank, data.worldbank.org/indicator/SP.DYN.TFRT.IN?locations=US

2. *'The Next Civil War by Stephen Marche; How Civil Wars Start by Barbara F Walter – review,'* The Guardian, 16 Jan 2022, theguardian.com/books/2022/jan/16/the-next-civil-war-stephen-marche-how-civil-wars-start-barbara-walter-review-nightmare-scenarios-for-the-us

3. Sir John Bagot Glubb, KCB, *'The Fate of Empires and Search for Survival,'* 1978, pg 12-14.

4. Eric Kaufmann, *'Shall the Religious Inherit the Earth?'* 2010, Location: 57, 71.

5. *Ibid.*, Introduction.

6. Sarah R. Hayford and S. Philip Morgan, *'Religiosity and Fertility in the United States: The Role of Fertility Intentions,'* Soc Forces, PMC 2009 Aug 10.

7. *'U.S. adults are more religious than Western Europeans,'* Pew Research Center, Sept 5, 2018, pewresearch.org/fact-tank/2018/09/05/u-s-adults-are-more-religious-than-western-europeans/

8. *'In U.S., Decline of Christianity Continues at Rapid Pace,'* Pew Research, 17 Oct 2019, pewforum.org/2019/10/17/in-u-s-decline-of-christianity-continues-at-rapid-pace/

9. Darrell Bricker and John Ibbitson, *'Empty Planet: The Shock of Global Population Decline,'* 2019, Location: 816, 824.

10. *Ibid.*, Location: 816, 824.

11. Eric Kaufmann, *'Shall the Religious Inherit the Earth?'* 2010, Location: 54, 57.

12. Prof Stein Emil Vollset, DrPH et al., *The Lancet,* 2020, thelancet.com/article/S0140-6736(20)30677-2/fulltext

13. *'The Jesus People Movement and The Charismatic Movement,'* PentecoStudies Vol. 10 No. 1 (2011). journal.equinoxpub.com/PENT/article/view/14218

14. *'Arnold Toynbee Talking About Religious Revival,'* BBC, youtube.com/watch?v=s3iq6VJx6T4

15. Sir John Bagot Glubb, KCB, *'The Fate of Empires and Search for Survival,'* 1978, pg 19.

Made in the USA
Las Vegas, NV
29 September 2022